Project Psychology

Project Psychology

Using Psychological Models and Techniques to Create a Successful Project

SHARON DE MASCIA
Chartered Business Psychologist

GOWER

Published by
Ashgate Publishing Limited
Wey Court East
Union Road
Farnham
Surrey, GU9 7PT
England

Ashgate Publishing Company
110 Cherry Street
Suite 3-1
Burlington
VT 05401-3818
USA

www.gowerpublishing.com

British Library Cataloguing in Publication Data
De Mascia, Sharon.
  Project psychology : using psychological models and
  techniques to create a successful project.
  1. Project management--Psychological aspects. 2. Personnel
  management--Psychological aspects.
  I. Title
  658.4'04'019-dc22

  ISBN: 978-0-566-08942-8 (hbk)
  IBSN: 978-1-4094-3829-8 (ebk)

Library of Congress Cataloging-in-Publication Data
De Mascia, Sharon.
  Project psychology : using psychological models and techniques to create a
  successful project / by Sharon De Mascia.
    p. cm.
  Includes bibliographical references and index.
  ISBN 978-0-566-08942-8 (hbk) -- ISBN 978-1-4094-3829-8
  (ebook) 1. Project management--Psychological aspects. 2. Teams in the
  workplace--Psychological aspects. I. Title.
  HD69.P75D399 2011
  658.4'04019--dc23

                                                                2011025338

Transferred to Digital Printing in 2014

Printed and bound in Great Britain
by Printondemand-worldwide.com

Contents

List of Figures

List of Tables

About the Author

Sharon De Mascia is the Director of 'Cognoscenti', a business Psychology Consultancy. www.cognoscenti.uk.com. She is a Chartered Business Psychologist and a HR/HRD professional. She has extensive project management experience and is Prince2 qualified as well as being an experienced Coach.

She has 20 years experience of delivering change management and other organisational initiatives across both public and private sectors. In the past she has worked with: Dorset Training and Enterprise Council, the NHS, Tyneside Training and Enterprise Council, The Employment Service, The Highways Agency, The Co-operative Insurance Society, The Vita Group, and Mendas.

Sharon is an assessor for the British Psychological Society and the Health Professions Council and an examiner for the International Baccalaureate in Psychology.

Reviews for
Project Psychology

This book delivers in detail what its title promises. It looks at all stages and process involved in project management and introduces methods and tools from Psychology (particularly Work and Occupational Psychology) that will aid success at each stage. It does not preach or condescend but allows the reader an opportunity to consider a range of approaches to people skills and people management which will allow the content of any project to be managed and led effectively.

The content is very accessible and each stage is self contained in an individual chapter. Tools and methods are introduced and reflective questions and useful illustrative tables guide the reader towards useful practice and a good understanding of what they can achieve by adopting the various approaches and specific tools. It is jargon free and is an excellent guide to the use of psychology in a practical setting by a non psychologist. It is a consultant in a book.

Dr P A Lindley, Chartered Psychologist and
Registered Occupational Psychologist

The principal factors in project success (and failure) are to do with people. Sharon De Mascia's book is a highly accomplished and relevant guide to getting the best out of people in projects. It deserves a place on the desk of anyone involved in a project – be they a sponsor, stakeholder, customer or project manager.

Eric Woodcock, CEng FRSA

Introduction

What is Project Management?

Projects vary considerably in terms of scale, cost, impact, duration and project management is basically an all-encompassing term which is used to describe the management of such projects. The list of what constitutes a project is endless and can range from having the office decorated to implementing a multi-million-pound global IT system. As one would imagine, there are many definitions of project management; however, the most definitive ones are those provided by the Office of Government and Commerce who developed 'Prince2' and the American Project Management Institute. The Prince2 definition of project management is: 'a management environment that is created for the purpose of delivering one or more business products according to the Business Case'. The definition provided by the American Project Management Institute is 'The application of knowledge, skills, tools and techniques to project activities to meet project requirements.'

In reality, there are a number of models that aim to provide support and consistency for project managers; however, they are very much focused on the mechanics of project delivery. It is important to recognise that project management models such as Prince2 are not intended to provide a full guide to project management but, in the words of Prince2 itself, solely 'contain a set of concepts and project management processes that are the minimum requirement for a properly run and managed project' (Prince2 manual).

Project management models such as Prince2 and that of the PMI do not include any guidance on how to deal with the two things that most projects have in common: firstly, they involve people, and secondly they bring about change for someone (Reiss 1992). These two factors are fundamental to the success of any project yet they are given only scant reference in the 'models' of project management that 'Project Managers are encouraged to follow'.

A number of the available models are rigorous and identify the nuts and bolts of project processes; however, they still fail to take account of the psychology of managing people and the psychology of managing change. These people factors are increasingly emerging as significant success factors in project management.

Briner (1992) comments that the world of traditional project management is evolving rapidly in fundamental ways. 'Firstly it is moving away from a preoccupation with planning and control tools as the key to success and towards the management of people and their performance'. This perception is echoed by Reiss (1992) who comments that projects generally involve people and they usually bring about change for someone. He then goes on to comment that 'Project Management is the management of change'.

I would agree entirely with Reiss's comment; however, in my experience, the change that Briner suggested does not appear to be happening. Prince2 and similar project management methodologies are based on sets of processes which are clear and fairly prescriptive, the idea being that if you put these processes in place, you will have a successful project. Given that the processes are fairly linear and mechanical in nature, they appear to be attracting non-people-oriented project managers, that is, people with IT and technical backgrounds. This can be very useful for IT projects; however, there appears to be a skill set missing which deals with people and managing the people-aspects of change. I believe that this is one of the reasons why a number of the big organisational-wide projects either fail completely or fail to realise the benefits that they set out to achieve.

I have been involved in assessing candidates for project management roles using psychometric assessments, and invariably the vast majority of the candidates lack a sufficient level of emotional intelligence, that is, they are not people-focused. This is a worrying trend as most change is about people and harnessing their energies. Project managers who understand the significance of the human element in projects and who know how to successfully address people-issues at all stages of the project cycle are more likely to be successful as project managers. This opinion is supported by emerging research into what makes projects successful.

Project management is a feature of modern-day organisational life and project management has emerged as a discipline in its own right. There is no shortage of projects waiting to be delivered and there will be few organisations that do not have several projects on the go at any time. A great deal of money is invested in these projects but unfortunately the chances of success do not appear to be good. Following research by the PA Consultancy Group in 2000, Kris Barrezeele suggests that 70 per cent of organisations across Benelux are consistently failing to deliver project work.

This is a rather depressing figure which I am sure has contributed to a motivation amongst researchers and practitioners alike to try to understand how to make a project successful. There has, however, been much debate with regard to what constitutes 'success' for a project (Cleland and King 1983). I would suggest that for the purpose of our discussion we assume that a successful project is one that has delivered all aspects of the project plan, within time and budget, whilst ensuring that sponsors and stakeholders are content with the quality of what has been delivered and that the delivered products or services are fit for purpose and sustainable.

Why Do Projects Fail?

> *A new HR computer system set to deliver multi-million pound savings for the Metropolitan Police is running six months late and £10 million pound over budget, according to reports. The system supplied by French IT Firm 'Steria' was designed to cost £38 million and become operational last December [2009]. (People Management 2010)*

According to Hylväri (2007) our current knowledge with regard to understanding the factors that enable project success is inadequate; however, there have been a number of studies carried out in this area (including Hylväri's own research) which are starting to shed some light on what makes projects successful and the factors that contribute to this success. Hylväri found that the experience of project managers, especially in change-management, was perceived as having great significance for project success, along with the ability to inspire/motivate people and to communicate well. There was also a perception that project managers needed to be decisive.

Zimmerer and Yasin (1998) found that in order for projects to be delivered successfully, it was necessary not only for project managers to be technically competent but also good leaders with the ability to lead by example and exercise vision. Hylväri also suggests that knowledge about small group dynamics established during the sixties and seventies is seldom used in project management, despite the fact that project management is about teams of people and influence.

Hylväri also suggests that 'Conflict Management' is a pre-requisite for project managers and cites research carried out by Yukl (2002) which found a significant correlation between the success of a project and the following leadership characteristics: planning, organising, networking, conflict management, team building factors and motivating/inspiring/developing.

Over and above the 'people' causes of project failure, there are other causes which tend to be around project delivery factors. The main ones are mentioned briefly here.

Barrezeele (2000) found four key areas that differentiated the companies that delivered projects well:

1. Effective project management with an emphasis on strong leadership and a structure project environment.

2. Good project definition at the outset, including, business benefits, timescales and so on.

3. Supportive sponsorship throughout the project and at a high level.

4. Effective change control that allowed sufficient flexibility to meet changing demands.

The Standish Group (1995) surveyed IT managers to elicit their opinions as to what makes projects successful and they identified three main factors that provide a project with a greater potential for success:

*   user involvement

*   executive management support

*   clear statement of requirements

There is a strong human element running through all of these project success factors, which underlines the significance of psychology to project management, which is the purpose of this book.

SUMMARY

The actual cost of project failure is extremely high both in monetary terms (given the amount of money invested on an annual basis) and human terms (given the damage to morale and so on that poor project management can create). This could be changed and the success rate of project management be increased if more psychological principles and practices were adopted in every phase of the project life cycle. It is clear that there are some things that are starting to emerge as significant factors in determining the success of a project – for example, strong leadership, management support, user engagement and a clear project brief. It is also clear, however, that a significant number of the reasons why projects fail are people-related. The science of psychology is about understanding the motivations and behaviours of people and applying that knowledge to a range of situations, including business environments. It stands to reason then that a science of human motivation and behaviour must have much to offer the discipline of project management.

What Can Psychology Offer to Project Managers to Ensure That Their Projects Have an Increased Chance of Success?

All projects involve people. Firstly there will be the project team, which could be simply two people or could be a huge global team. Secondly there will be stakeholders for the project and there will probably be suppliers for the project and ultimately other people who are affected by what the project is trying to achieve. The varying needs of these people need to be taken into account and properly managed if the project is to be successful. This could include a number of measures:

- ensuring that an appropriately skilled project team is selected so that the right people with the right skills are in the correct roles

- ensuring that that the project manager and the project team not only have the skills needed to produce and manage a project plan but also the skill of leading people

- creating a real project team that bonds together in pursuit of a common aim and continues to work as one throughout the duration of the project

- ensuring that the needs of stakeholders are understood and ensuring that there is psychological buy in for their time

- ensuring that stakeholders are engaged and involved in a way that is meaningful to them and creates a bond between them and the project team

- communicating effectively and setting clear goals so that everyone understands their role in the project

- understanding how to negotiate with stakeholders and effectively manage any emerging conflict

- understanding how to best manage project risks and, where appropriate, bring about sustainable organisational change

This book aims to provide you with an understanding of the contribution that psychology can make to ensuring that your projects have a higher chance of being successful.

What the Book Will Be Covering in Each of the Subsequent Chapters

Chapter 1 of the book looks at the types of skills and attitudes that are needed by both the project manager and the project team generally. It then goes on to look at research into project teams and how they differ from the usual teams that are found in organisations. It explores the implications that the research has for the types of skills and attitudes required in a successful project team. The chapter ends by looking at how these skills and attitudes can be measured in order to successfully choose project team members. It looks at ways of effectively selecting those skills using psychometric tests and assessment methodologies.

The second chapter looks at project leadership and briefly explores some of the more popular leadership models that might be appropriate for a project manager in managing a project team. It explores some of the older models such as the 'Blake Mouton grid' which focuses on dimensions of task and people and the Hershey and Blanchard Lifecycle approach which recognises that leadership is a two-way process and that project team members can influence the type of leadership that is necessary. The chapter then starts to look at some of the more recent and emerging models of leadership that focus on emotional intelligence and building trusting relationships with project team members in order to motivate and engage them.

Chapter 3 is about building a strong cohesive team that will give your project the best possible chance of succeeding. It commences by looking at some of the characteristics of teams and linking these back into the leadership models that we explored in the previous chapter. It looks at the roles that people habitually play within teams using models such as 'Belbin's team roles' and uses the 'Myers Briggs' model and 'Transactional Analysis' to explore how people relate to each other in teams. It then proceeds to look at using positive psychology to energise a project team. The chapter ends by exploring team culture and climate. It looks at the factors involved in creating an environment that facilitates high performing teams whilst being psychologically healthy and motivating. There is also a brief discussion of some of the more negative processes that can occur in teams and why these should be avoided at all costs.

In Chapter 4, we look at 'coaching' and how it can be a useful tool for project managers. The chapter explores how a coaching style can be used to motivate and empower staff as well as developing them. It provides another method of helping to improve team performance. The first part of this chapter explores coaching as a leadership style and looks at the underlying skills necessary in order to successfully utilise a coaching approach to leadership. The chapter looks at applying one of the most popular coaching models to project management and demonstrates how it could be used. The chapter then finishes with an exploration of team coaching.

Chapter 5 explores the relationship between the project team and stakeholders. It looks at why it is important to ensure that stakeholders are engaged in the project and how best to engage them. It details some of the methods that project managers can use to achieve this. The chapter continues by looking at using 'goal setting' techniques to ensure that stakeholders are clear about various aspects of the project and their role within it. The chapter then looks at how to engage in positive negotiation with stakeholders in order to ensure that good relationships are maintained whilst achieving project aims and objectives. Finally, the chapter looks briefly at how a coaching approach can be successfully used with stakeholders in order to build and maintain good relationships.

Chapter 6 looks at communications and the contribution that psychology can make to the production of a successful communication plan. Communication is vital when delivering projects and this chapter looks at some of the underlying factors that need to be taken into account when producing a communication strategy for a project. Chapter 6 looks briefly at some of the methodologies of communication that are available now and then proceeds to look at communication as an aspect of human behaviour and explores our perceptions, cognitions and emotions with regard to the process of communicating. The chapter also looks at non-verbal aspects of communication and then closes by looking at how 'Transactional Analysis' can be used to facilitate good communication.

Research has shown that people are more likely to take risks where they feel supported, there is a no-blame culture and they are trusted/empowered to take those risks. Human beings differ immensely in the extent to which they are prepared to take risks and the enormity of the risks that they are prepared to take. The management of risk is a key task for any project manager and it is worth having a deeper understanding of the contribution that personality makes to the experience of risk. In Chapter 7 the topic of 'project risk' is explored and, given that much has already been written on this topic, this chapter concentrates on risk from a more human angle and explores the psychology of risk. The chapter looks at the three elements of human behaviour that need to be considered in association with any risk management process: individual factors, group factors and organisational factors. The chapter ends by suggesting some actions that project managers can take in order to better manage project risk.

Unfortunately, project management has a huge propensity for conflict simply because there are numerous independent relationships and projects often cross organisational and managerial boundaries. In addition, the often tight time-constraints of project activities can bring project teams into conflict with stakeholders who also have to deliver day-to-day business as well. Chapter 8 explores the four different types of conflict – interpersonal, intrapersonal, intragroup and intergroup – and looks at how these different types of conflict can manifest themselves. The chapter then looks at addressing conflict and explores how conflict can be as much a positive force as a negative one. It looks at how conflict can be used in a positive way to bring about growth and development.

There are numerous academic texts and research papers on the subject of change management and many models have been developed to facilitate effective change. Research into change management has proven that there are certain circumstances that have to be present for effective change to take place. At its simplest level this involves people being fully informed about the change and being involved with it in a meaningful way. Change is not brought about by simply changing processes; one has to create a culture of involvement and sharing so that people actually buy into and utilise the new processes.

The psychology of change management has much to offer a project manager in terms of making his/her project more successful. Consequently, Chapter 9 looks at change management and how to implement a successful strategy for change in a project plan. The chapter starts by looking at individual reactions to change and then looks at how best to address these within an organisational context. There is then a discussion around how to bring about organisational change and how to ensure that the change is sustainable in the longer term.

The project board is there as a resource to the project manager but a number of project managers experience relatively poor relationships with their project board. Chapter 10 looks at some of the common issues found with project boards and explores what actions can be taken to overcome these difficulties. There is also a section on building good relationships with the project board so that it acts as a resource to the project manager. In addition, this chapter looks at how to protect yourself as a project manager when others fail to cooperate.

From the relatively high percentage of failed projects, it would appear that a large number of organisations do not learn from their failures, or at least do not learn enough from them to prevent reoccurrences. Chapter 11 looks at why it is important that organisations learn from their failed projects and explores the concept of 'organisational learning' in general and how Kolb's (1984) model of learning can be used to implement some good organisational practices. This chapter also examines 'organisational defensiveness' routines and explores the role that leaders and the organisational environment play in whether or not organisations learn from their project failures. There are suggestions for measures that project managers (and organisations) can put in place to ensure that they capture sufficient information from projects to allow them to capture and disseminate valuable learning.

In Chapter 12 we will look at how best to manage team feelings about the end of the project and the dissolution of the team. We will also look at what additional actions need to be taken at the end of the project in order to ensure that maximum learning is taken from the experience and that the changes that have been brought about are sustainable.

1

The Project Team: Skills and Attitudes

Identifying the Skills/Attitudes of the Project Team and Selecting the Project Team

This chapter of the book looks at the types of skills and attitudes that you are likely to need from both a project manager and a project team. It looks at skills and attributes required and how they have changed in the light of the changing project environment and recent research into what makes projects successful. It also looks at some of the differences between the skills required for general teams and those required for project teams. This chapter ends with a brief look at ways of helping you select the right project team.

What Are the Skills And Attitudes Normally Associated with Being a Project Manager?

The earlier project management literature tends to focus on the differences between line managers and project managers for example; there is an emphasis on project management as a discrete short-term entity.

Table 1.1   The differences between project managers and line managers

PROJECT MANAGEMENT	LINE MANAGEMENT
A narrower focus aimed at delivering a short-term project. This would involve building close working relationships in order to meet project milestones	A broader, long-term focus on organisational performance. This would involve general management in order to achieve broader organisational objectives

However, these boundaries have blurred over time and twenty-first-century projects can last for many years with multiple strands or foci to them. Consequently, it is probably more helpful to look at the types of skills and attributes that are essential for a project manager.

Meredith and Mantel (2003) suggest a list of skills and attributes that they perceived to be popular in the selection of project managers:

- a strong technical background

- a hard-nosed manager

- a mature individual

- someone who is currently available

- someone who is on good terms with senior management

- someone who can keep the project team happy

- someone who has worked in several departments

- someone who can walk on water

Most of us will have witnessed some of these criteria on show in various organisations; however, in themselves, they are unlikely to increase the potential success of the project. Lientz and Rea (2000) also describe a list of attributes that they feel are essential to project managers. The list has much in common with that provided by Meredith and Mantel (2003) with the addition of 'being a good problem solver', 'being energetic and ambitious', 'being a risk taker' and finally, 'having a sense of humour'.

Meredith and Mantel (2003) quote a survey reported by Posner (1987) in the *Project Management Journal*. Posner asked project managers to complete a questionnaire which asked about the skills required to be a project manager. The results from the questionnaire suggested that project managers should have good communication skills and be able to listen and persuade. They should have good leadership skills so that they can create a positive vision and act as a role model. The results also suggested that project managers need good organisational and coping skills; along with team building and technological skills. As expected, there is a lot of commonality in what we have seen so far.

Gok (1997) carried out some research with project managers (all were full members of the UK Association of Project Managers) and he found that his participants identified 14 attributes that were important for project managers. These characteristics fell into four categories:

- the ability to meet project deadlines

- human related abilities

- personal traits

- technical ability

Examples of attributes within these categories included: being recognised as a team player, ability to manage budgets and so on. Having looked at the attributes identified by Meredith and Mantel (2003), Lientz and Rea (2000) and Posner (1987) they could all be subsumed under categories identified by Gok (1997); however, like most things, the devil is in the detail. A comparison of the various lists of attributes reveals that there are many similarities between them, particularly those produced by Lientz and Rea and Posner and the attributes cited are those which anyone would be hard pushed to disagree with, for example communication, the ability to motivate, vision, organisational skills and energy. There are, however, some differences; for example, the Lientz and Rea list refers to risk-taking which is lacking in the Posner list whilst the Posner emphasises team-building skills. Let's explore what light, if any, recent research into project success factors and psychological research generally sheds on these lists of attributes.

Attributes That Have Been Found to Contribute to Project Success in the Twenty-First Century

The findings reported in the previous chapter (Hylväri 2007, Yukl 2002, Zimmerer and Yasin 1998, Barrezeele 2000) suggest that the following attributes in project managers are significantly associated with successful projects.

- *Experience in change management* – this was considered to have great significance for project success. It is important when delivering a project to be able to manage both the technical elements and the people elements of a project. As we have already said, projects are about change so it stands to reason that a project team which understands the fundamentals of achieving change is more likely to succeed than their less experienced counterparts.

- *Leadership ability* – Zimmerer and Yasin (1998) found that 76 per cent of project success could be attributed to positive leadership, for example being visionary, leading by example and also being technically competent.

- *Ability to inspire and motivate people* – this is tied in with leadership skills, in that, the project manager's ability to motivate and inspire the project team and stakeholders has been identified as a significant factor in project success.

- *Team building/developing* – the ability of the project manager to build and develop the skills of the project team has also been identified as a crucial factor in project success. This also an understanding of group dynamics, that is, how individuals in groups/teams relate to each other and to those outside the immediate group/team.

- *Good communicator* – project managers need to be able to inspire and motivate people. The ability to communicate effectively is fundamental to this. Political awareness and sensitivity were also found to be significant factors.

- *Good decision-maker* – projects involve decision-making and the project manager needs to be able to make timely, effective decisions even if the decision is to delegate the decision upwards or sideways.

- *Good conflict manager* – projects often depend on matrix management and a range of stakeholders so it is not surprising that conflict occurs from time to time. Equally it is hardly surprising that the ability to manage conflict has emerged as a critical skill for project managers.

- *The ability to create a structured project environment* – along with good planning/networking, organisational skills were found to be significant factors in the effective delivery of projects.

This list does not purport to be an exhaustive one; it merely contains the attributes that have been demonstrated to have a link with successful performance. It is probably worth looking at some of these areas in more detail and we will continue exploring some of these 'success factor' attributes throughout subsequent chapters.

In my experience, the existence of Prince2 and other easily accessible models for delivering projects is creating a trend for project managers coming from certain backgrounds and to have certain skill sets. Prince2 and similar project-management methodologies are based on sets of processes which are clear and fairly prescriptive, the idea being that if you put these processes in place, you will have a successful project. Given that the processes are fairly linear and mechanical they appear to be attracting non-people-oriented project managers – that is, people with IT and technical backgrounds who are, no doubt, attracted by the current image of project management as a set of linear and logical processes to be delivered in a predetermined sequence. This can be very useful for IT projects; however, in my experience, there appears to be a skill set missing around dealing with people and managing the people aspects of change and I believe that this is one of the reasons why a number of the big expensive projects either fail completely or fail to realise the benefits that they set out to achieve. Consequently, as well as the skills identified above, I would also include emotional intelligence, risk-taking preferences, engagement ability, coaching ability, integrity, personal resilience and goal setting. We will go on to look at these skills in more detail throughout subsequent chapters.

What Skills and Attitudes Do You Need from a Project Team?

Within society there are many different groupings of people. A team is one particular type of group. Moxon (1993) suggests that a team has the following attributes:

- a common purpose

- recognition by each individual as belonging to the same unit, that is, team identity

- interdependent functions

- agreed norms or values which regulate behaviour

Project teams have some complexities that are not always present in other types of teams. To take one example, project teams usually have a limited existence as they are exist for the duration of the project. Secondly, they are often matrix-managed which means that some (or all) team members may have a manager for their day job and the project manager for that portion of their work that relates to the project. This can cause conflicts for both the project manager and the project team. An additional complication is that, as for a number of teams today, project teams are often not co-located physically and may be spread across the country or even the world. These additional complexities make it even more necessary that the project manager invest time in building his/her team, which we will go on to talk about in Chapter 3.

Team Member Skills

The number of people in a project team and the variety of specialisms that they possess will vary considerably according to the nature, scope and value of the project. A small project may only have two or three members, whereas a larger-scale project could have hundreds.

Some projects will require more specialist skills than others. In my experience, when delivering IT projects it is essential to have appropriate knowledge and experience in the project team around existing systems, relevant software, requirements of any new system and knowledge of interfaces and user requirements. Similarly in HR-related projects, it is essential to have someone who understands how current HR policies and procedures work and what impact the project will have on those. Regardless of the degree of specialist knowledge needed, however, there are some underlying attributes that are necessary in every project team if it is to be successful.

There is considerably less in the literature generally on the skills associated with being a project team member than there is on being a project manager; however, even the best project manager will struggle to succeed if he or she lacks the appropriate skills and knowledge within the project team. Consequently, it is just as important look at the sorts of skills that you require in your project team members; over and above any specialist skills as mentioned above. I think it is fair to say that most project team members will need the same types of skills to be a project team member as they do to be a member of other types of organisational teams. There are, however, certain skills which are more strongly emphasised in project teams simply due to the nature of project management itself.

Tyson, Mills, Finn and Stevenson (2009) carried out a piece of research to identify the skills that facilitated high-performing teams and they found 16 competencies across four clusters which are detailed in Table 1.2. They found that the four clusters contributed to two key drivers of performance that is, the capacity to create a collective ability to deliver the task and the ability to create an environment in which teams were able to deliver to a high standard. They looked at a variety of different types of teams (including project teams) and found that certain competencies were more important for some teams than others, depending on the degree of task structure (that is, high or low) and the stability (or not) of team membership.

Project teams tend to be characterised by an unstable team membership as people enter and leave the project and by a high task-structure as projects are task focused. Consequently, there are some skills that are more important for project teams than for other teams generally. Consequently, project team members will need to possess higher levels of communication and influencing skills than would necessarily be required for other team memberships. This is for several reasons. Firstly, project team members are ambassadors for the project and will often be in a position of having to gain support for the project whether it is trying to win over people from their own departments (in a matrix model) or trying to convince people outside the project to engage in

Table 1.2   Team skills

Enabling	Fusing
Communicating and integrating Adapting and being situationally aware Evolving expertise and being creative	Emotional maturation Bonding Openness Affiliating
Resourcing	**Motivating**
Knowing Being able to put things into context Having team wisdom	Being committed Being inspired Being a believer

certain behaviours. Secondly, team members will also need the ability to build relationships and bond with the rest of the project team and people outside the project team. This means that they will need a certain amount of emotional intelligence, which is about being interpersonally sensitive to the needs of others (we will look at this in more detail in the next chapter). One could argue that the ability to build relationships is an essential requirement for any team member; however, it can be more crucial in project teams owing to their less permanent nature and potentially wider, more complex range of stakeholders.

Team members will also need to be flexible and open to experience as projects can be very volatile and people often need to be able to amend project plans and activities at the drop of a hat. In my experience, team members who enjoy a high degree of stability in their work do not fare well in project teams and find the constant task fluctuation too stressful.

Project team members will also need to be able to operate with minimum supervision, as with 'fast paced' project teams it is not always possible to closely supervise staff. This fluidity of project teams often means that support is not readily available to team members in the way that it can be in more stable, permanent teams. This means that project team members also need to be supportive of their fellow project team members and be good at situational sensing, that is be able to keep a collective eye on the bigger picture and monitor team performance.

Project team members will also need good organisational skills in order not only to ensure that projects run to schedule but also to ensure that they are able to juggle operational demands alongside the demands of planning, monitoring and evaluating which usually accompany projects. In my experience, project team members who are unable to think logically and understand that 'events' within a project are usually interdependent and therefore need to be delivered to a timed sequence create an additional level of risk and can put the project in jeopardy.

In addition, it is helpful for project team members to have some degree of financial knowledge. They do not have to be accountants, as most projects will have someone with financial expertise keeping an overall eye on spending; however, all project members will have a degree of control over one or more aspects of a project plan and at the very least they will need to be able to consider the financial implications when making decisions. It is probably fair to assume that project team members will require a sub-set of the skills required to be a project manager.

Project work can sometimes lead to people feeling a little isolated as they may be taken out of their usual teams and included in a project team which may be virtual or non-co-located. This all adds to the pressure of the role and team members will need to possess a certain amount of personal resilience, particularly where they have to report to a manager for their day job and the project manager for project work. This isolation and blurring of reporting lines can prove to be too much for some project members and it is important when recruiting team members to ensure that they are in no doubt about the more open structures that project team members have to work within. Project team members also have to work much harder at understanding the expertise that other team members have and also their weaknesses, because they do not have the luxury of time that teams with more a more stable membership have. It is important that both the project team member and the project manager are assertive in ensuring that sufficient time is allocated to the project as opposed to the day job.

In summary then, there are no distinct skill sets for project team members; however, there are differences in the levels of certain skills needed and it is important to bear this in mind when selecting your project team.

Selecting a Project Manager and Project Team

The field of psychology offers a range of tools and techniques to assist in the selection of an effective project team, for example by using psychometric tests.

What Are Psychometric Tests?

Psychometric tests are objective tests which aim to measure one or more areas of human behaviour. Psychometric tests are standardised, which is to say they utilise a common administrative procedure and scoring mechanism for all candidates on each occasion that they are used. They are generally based on years of research and the best ones are approved by the British Psychological Society as being both reliable and valid selection tools. Psychometric tests aim to be fair and not to disadvantage any group or individual.

Psychological tests are commonly used in employment situations both as coaching aids and to select and develop people (Anastasi 1990). There are several different types of psychometric tests – for example, aptitude tests (clerical skills, IT skills), ability tests (verbal, numerical), interest/motivation inventories, culture/climate inventories and personality measures/emotional intelligence. They can only be utilised by people who have completed the appropriate level of training identified by the British Psychological Society who regulate the quality and usage of such measures (www.BPS.org.uk). Your HR department should be able to help you with this.

What Can Psychometric Tests Contribute to the Selection of Project Managers and Project Teams?

A number of the skills and attributes required in project managers and project teams that we identified earlier could be more accurately identified using psychometric measures, so let us go on to look at some of the measures that might be of assistance in selecting a project team.

Personality Measures

Personality measures have evolved as a result of over 50 years of research and the most well-known ones tend to be based around the 'Big Five' factors of personality that have been identified consistently by many researchers (Barrick and Mount 1991). The five factors are:

- extraversion – traits frequently associated with this include being sociable, gregarious, assertive, talkative and active

- emotional stability – traits frequently associated with this include being calm, emotionally stable, and having a degree of personal resilience

- openness to experience – traits frequently associated with this include being imaginative, curious, original, broad minded, and artistically sensitive

- conscientiousness – traits frequently associated with this include being careful, dependable, organised, persevering

- agreeableness – traits frequently associated with this include being courteous, flexible, trusting, good-natured, cooperative, forgiving, soft-hearted and tolerant

There are a number of personality measures that could be utilised to assess the project management skills identified earlier; however, there are too many to be discussed here. Available personality measures include the Occupational Personality Questionnaire (Saville and Holdsworth), the 16PF (IPAT), Wave (Saville Consulting), PAPI, to name but a few.

The accuracy of the assessment could be further strengthened through the addition of other assessment measures, for example the addition of questionnaires to assess verbal and numerical reasoning. Assessment centre methodology is often used to select people. Assessment centres tend to be half- or full-day events in which potential candidates engage in a variety of activities (related to the job that they are being selected for) whilst being observed and assessed by trained assessors. Assessment centres typically utilise a range of measures, for example psychometric tests, personality measures, in-tray exercises, group exercises and so on. They are all designed to assess the candidate's suitability against the competencies identified for the job. Properly constructed assessment centres are very accurate predictors; however, they can be relatively costly to establish and run and may be impractical if a project team is being selected only for a short, inexpensive project. In these instances, it might be better to use a simpler combination of measures, for example psychometric tests and interviews.

Questions for Reflection

1. What skills and attitude do you think that you will need in order to deliver your project successfully?

2. What skills and attitude do you need from your project team in order to deliver this project successfully?

3. What personality traits will you need in order to deliver the project successfully?

4. What personality traits will you need in your project team?

5. How will you select your project team?

6. What resources will you need to select the team and where will you find them?

2

What Sort of Leader Should a Project Manager Be?

Once the project manager is in post he will have selected the project team or inherited it as sometimes is the case. The success of the project will obviously depend on a number of factors; however, the efficacy of the project manager and the project team are important factors in the success of the project. Project teams can be even more complicated to manage than the average organisational team for a number of reasons. Firstly, the team can be relatively short lived, depending on the duration of the project, so there is not the same luxury of time to build the team. Secondly, often a high percentage of the staff employed on a project (if not all) will have a real job to do as well as delivering the project and may only be matrix managed by the project manager. This means that the project manager will have to ensure that his team's individual managers are included in the stakeholder analysis and that there is a plan in hand to inform and engage this group. We will go on to look at this in more detail in the second part of this book; when we look at the project planning stage. These additional potential complexities make it even more important to ensure that the project team is effectively engaged and motivated.

Styles of Project Leadership

There are many theories of leadership and rather than explore an exhaustive list of different models of leadership, we will look instead at several aspects of leadership that appear to be most relevant to project management. Pinto et al. (1998) comment that 'Project management is a leader-intensive undertaking' and, as we have already seen from the research explored earlier, strong leadership is essential to the success of projects. Consequently the question of what type of leadership is needed is a crucial question in any leadership task.

We are going to look at the following models of leadership which appear to have the most relevance for project managers:

- the managerial grid

- situational leadership

- transformational leadership

- emotionally intelligent leadership

- authentic leadership

People-Orientation or Task-Orientation?

David Cleland (1990) suggests that the characteristics of successful project teams can be divided into two categories, that is, people-oriented characteristics and task/result-oriented characteristics. Similarly, there is a leadership model that is also focused on the compromise between task focus and people focus (the managerial grid) and it is probably worth having a cursory look at it. The managerial grid (Figure 2.1) was conceived by Blake and Mouton (1966) reported in Luthans (1989) and it aims to identify leadership styles in practice.

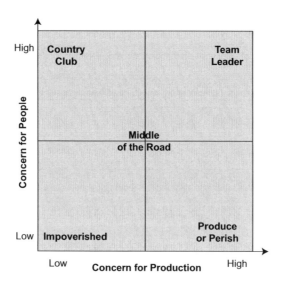

Figure 2.1   The managerial grid

The managerial grid has two axes. The vertical axis represents 'Concern for People' and the horizontal axis represents 'Concern for Production' or task. Blake and Mouton (1966) suggest that there are five styles of leadership (explained below) depending on where someone fits on the managerial grid. The five different kinds of leadership are 'Impoverished', 'Team Leader', 'Middle-of-the-Road', 'Country Club' and 'Produce or Perish'. The 'Country Club' (people orientation) and the 'Task Manager' (task orientation) represent the two extremes of the grid with the former being totally focused on the people (at the expense of the tasks) and the 'Task Manager' is totally focused on the tasks at the expense of the people. The other categories fall in between these two, although 'Team Leader' is cited as the most effective type of leadership. Different leadership styles may be appropriate with different projects or at different points within the project life cycle which suggests that the 'Situational' models of leadership can offer a useful perspective.

The Different Types of Leadership Proposed in the Managerial Grid

IMPOVERISHED LEADERSHIP (LOW ON THE 'PRODUCTION' AXIS AND LOW ON THE 'PEOPLE' AXIS)

A project manager using this leadership style would generally be ineffective. This style is characterised by someone who is trying to preserve his status and avoid any mistakes being made that could threaten either his security or status within the organisation. The low concern for either people or delivering against project objectives is likely to result in a low level of achievement and discontented team members.

TEAM LEADER (HIGH ON THE 'PRODUCTION' AXIS AND HIGH ON THE 'PEOPLE' AXIS)

This was considered to be the best leadership style by Blake and Mouton. Project managers utilising this leadership style would be equally concerned for the welfare and happiness of the team and the need to deliver against project objectives. The assumption behind this leadership style is that team members want to be involved in determining how the project is delivered and will feel happier and be more productive as a result.

MIDDLE-OF-THE-ROAD LEADERSHIP (MEDIUM ON THE 'PRODUCTION' AXIS AND MEDIUM ON THE 'PEOPLE' AXIS)

A project manager who utilised this style would appear to be trying to get the best balance possible between delivering against project objectives whilst trying to demonstrate concern for the welfare of the team. The only problem with trying to achieve a balance in this way is that any balance achieved will always be a compromise and may not be the most efficient way to lead or the most effective.

THE COUNTRY CLUB LEADER (HIGH ON THE PEOPLE AXIS BUT LOW ON THE 'PRODUCTION' AXIS)

This leadership style is where the project manager is very concerned about the welfare of the team but less focused on delivery, that is, there is a lack of direction and control. This style is characterised by someone who believes that if team members are happy then they will work hard; consequently there is no need for him to worry about anything other than the team's happiness. A project managed by a leader utilising this leadership would probably result in a nice and pleasant work environment but would probably struggle to deliver much against project objectives.

PRODUCE OR PERISH LEADERSHIP (HIGH ON THE 'PRODUCTION' AXIS AND 'LOW ON THE 'PEOPLE' AXIS)

Project managers utilising this leadership style would appear very authoritarian. The focus would be on delivery at all costs and the well-being and happiness of the team would be very much a secondary consideration.

A NOTE OF CAUTION FOR PROJECT MANAGERS

It is probably also worth adding a note of caution here for project managers, particularly those that come from a non-people-focused background. Because projects are all about deliverables and timescales it is sometimes very easy to be seduced by the glory of focusing on the project plan and the many tasks that have to be delivered. It is very important to constantly remind yourself that every additional moment that you are focused on tasks is one less moment focused on the people side of the equation, which is usually the most unpredictable and volatile element of the whole project management equation.

SOME QUESTIONS FOR REFLECTION

1. How important is it that the tasks are delivered and within what timescales?

2. How clear are the project team about their individual objectives and deliverables within the project?

3. To what extent (and in what circumstances) do you tend to focus more on 'tasks' than 'people' and vice versa?

4. When you feel that it is imperative to focus on 'tasks'? how do you take an 'emotion check' in order to know how the team are thinking and feeling?

5. When you feel that it is important to focus on the 'people' element, how do you ensure that the relevant tasks are delivered?

6. What steps could you take to ensure that you find the optimum balance between managing the 'tasks' and managing the emotional and support needs of project team members?

SITUATIONAL LEADERSHIP

'Situational Leadership', as the name suggests, is based on the premise that the style of leadership needed will vary according to situational variables, for example the relationship between the leader and his co-workers. One such situational model is Hersey and Blanchard's life cycle approach.

The Hersey and Blanchard's Life Cycle Approach

This model of leadership builds on both on the managerial grid and on research carried out by Fred Fiedler in Luthans (1998) that looks at the impact of situational variables on overall team performance. Similar to the managerial grid, the Hersey and Blanchard model identifies leadership styles associated with, one the one hand, tasks and on the other, relationships; however, it goes a little further and introduces a third variable of follower maturity. Follower maturity is, in essence, the extent to which project team members are willing/unwilling to take responsibility, their level of experience/education and how motivated they are. Hersey and Blanchard suggest that the leader will need to adopt different levels of participation and authority according to where the follower or team member is in comparison with the three criteria.

Hersey and Blanchard described the various alternative leadership styles that the leader may adopt as telling style, selling style, participating style and delegating style. Pinto et al. (1998) describe Hersey and Blanchard's model in project management terms and provide the following examples of what each of Hersey and Blanchard's styles might look like for a project manager.

TELLING

Appropriate with team members who lack the relevant motivation, skills and so on to perform well. The team member will require clear instruction and regular intervention from the project manager.

SELLING

This style is deemed necessary when team members are motivated to do well but lack the necessary abilities. This team member will require some instruction.

PARTICIPATING

This style is deemed suitable where team members are very capable but may lack the motivation to perform well. Here the project manager will need to intervene to increase the team member's confidence levels.

DELEGATING

Where team members are motivated and capable there will be little need for intervention by the project manager.

Pinto et al. (1998) suggest that a project manager's ability to lead effectively relies on an understanding of alternative approaches to leadership. They need to be practical and flexible enough to be able to change their leadership style in accordance with what is happening around them. I think it is probably fair to say that the ability to flex leadership styles is crucial to success in all leadership and not just when leading projects. In 2009, Hersey, Blanchard and Johnson further developed their theory to accommodate the development level of followers, which they referred to as the 'Performance Readiness Level'.

They identified the following stages which portray the individual's learning journey from enthusiastic beginner to confident and motivated performer.

- R1 – Unable and Insecure or Unwilling – where the follower is unable and insecure or lacks confidence.

- R2 – Unable but Confident or Willing – where the follower is unable to complete tasks but is confident as long as the leader provides the appropriate guidance.

- R3 – Able but Insecure or Unwilling – where the follower has the ability to complete tasks but is apprehensive about performing alone or is not willing to use his/her ability.

- R4 – Able but Confident and Willing – where the follower has the ability to perform and is confident about completing tasks.

SOME QUESTIONS FOR REFLECTION

1. To what extent is each of your project team members confident and experienced?

2. To what extent is each team member capable of delivering his role and what level of development is required?

3. Are team members suitably motivated?

4. What does each of them need from you, in terms of, practical and emotional support?

5. How do you relate to the team and how do they relate to you? For example, are you the boss who tells each of them what to do or do they work autonomously and only come to you when they need more authority to make something happen?

6. What is your habitual style of communicating with your team? For example, do you prefer to tell or consult?

7. What percentage of each project team member's objectives are about their learning and development?

8. How will you create opportunities to develop and grow project team members?

TRANSFORMATIONAL LEADERSHIP

Transformational leadership is another leadership model that is highly relevant to project management. Transformational leaders bring about change at an organisational level by creating a vision and engaging staff and stakeholders to contribute to that vision (Burns, 1978). They are seen as change agents. Transformational leaders understand enough about the needs of their individual team members to be able to utilise those needs to help motivate the team. They are also able to use individual motivation to increase the overall motivational levels of the team. Transformational leaders are also able to inspire trust in those that they work with. Kouzes and Posner (1995) found that the chief characteristics possessed by effective leaders were honesty and integrity. Pinto et al. (1998) describe transformational leaders as having the following characteristics:

- *Vision* – Successful project managers offer their team members and stakeholders a view of where the project is heading and what success will look like.

- *Communication skills* – Successful project managers are able to communicate well to inform and inspire their teams and stakeholders.

- *Inspire trust* – The ability to instil a feeling of trust in project team members and stakeholders.

- *Ability to empower* – Transformational leaders are able to build confidence in their team members and encourage them to develop.

- *Energy and action orientation* – They have lots of energy and use their own positive outlook to influence others.

- *Emotional expression and warmth* – Transformational leaders are confident and are able to be open with people and express warmth appropriately.

- *Risk takers* – Transformational leaders understand that there are occasions when risks have to be taken in order to make major changes.

- *Think outside the box* – Transformational leaders look for creative solutions to problems and new and better ways of doing things.

QUESTIONS TO ASK YOURSELF

1. Do you have a vision for this project?

2. Are you passionate about that vision?

3. Do you share that vision with your project team members (including stakeholders) in a way that engages and enthuses them?

4. Do you know each project team member and his strengths/ aspirations well enough to allocate work in a way that motivates and engages them?

5. To what extent do you trust your team and to what extent do they trust you?

6. Do you generally behave in a positive and warm manner when you are with your team members?

7. To what extent do you share your feelings with your team members?

8. Do you take time to consider the impact that your behaviour and attitudes have on the team and the extent to which they may motivate or demotivate the team?

9. To what extent do you innovate in the way that you manage and deliver projects and to what extent do you encourage your team to take risks?

EMOTIONALLY INTELLIGENT LEADERSHIP

Research suggests that the higher you climb up the organisational ladder, the more crucial emotional intelligence or 'EI' becomes (Goleman et al. 2002).

Salovey and Mayor (1990) defined emotional intelligence as 'a form of social intelligence that involves the ability to monitor one's own and others' feelings and emotions, to discriminate among them and to use this information to guide one's thinking and action'.

Emotional intelligence is the foundation or bedrock from which we develop emotional intelligence competencies which are the personal and social skills which enable high or outstanding performance in the workplace.

EI is not only about knowing how and when to express emotion; it is also about influencing the emotions of those around us; which is why it is so crucial for leadership. Studies carried out over the years have demonstrated how the emotions of one key person in a group very quickly transmit to the others. Bachman (1988) found that the most effective leaders in the US navy were warmer, more outgoing, emotionally expressive, dramatic and sociable. It is not difficult to see that a team where the leader is enthusiastic and positive is more likely to achieve great things than a team where everyone is anxious and uncertain as a result of a negative and pessimistic team leader. EI is particular important for project managers because most projects are about change. Project managers need to be aware of and manage their own emotions so that they are then able to tune in and influence the emotions of those around them, bearing in mind that emotions can run high in times of change.

Table 2.1   The four components of emotional intelligence

Personal competence	Self-awareness
Self-awareness Self-management	Emotional self-awareness Accurate self-assessment Self-confidence
Social competence	**Self-management**
Social awareness Relationship management	Self-control Trustworthiness Conscientious Adaptability Achievement drive Initiative

Project managers can use emotionally intelligent leadership to ensure good performance and increase their chances of delivering a successful project. This can be achieved by harnessing the collective emotions of the project team and driving them in a positive direction. Goleman et al. (2002) describes this as 'Resonant Leadership'. The flip side of this kind of leaderships is what he calls 'Dissonant Leadership'. This occurs when leaders are not tuned in to the emotions of the group and are therefore not taking these into account when interacting with and leading the group. I am sure that we could all think of at least one example from our own personal experience where we have worked in a team that appears to be at odds with the team leader. There are various questionnaires available that purport to measure 'Emotional Intelligence', for example MSCEIT, Baron EQI, Goleman ECI 360.

QUESTIONS FOR REFLECTION

1. What percentage of the time am I aware of my own emotions?

2. To what extent do I allow my team to know what I am feeling or the depth of that emotion?

3. To what extent am I aware of what my team members are feeling at time?

4. Do I allow what I am feeling to influence the way in which I interact with my team members or stakeholders?

5. To what extent do I use my awareness of how team members or stakeholders are feeling, to influence how I behave towards them or how I interact with them?

6. To what extent do I feel that I am 'in tune' with my project team?

AUTHENTIC LEADERSHIP

Authentic leadership is a relatively emerging concept in leadership and it defines a type of leadership that is value-based and aimed at motivating and engaging people. It has some similarities with the transformational leadership model and emotionally intelligent model that we looked at earlier. It also relates to the 'positive strengths' approach that we will be looking at in the next chapter.

Authentic leadership is not so much a model but an underlying set of values. It is about being yourself and being true to yourself regardless of which leadership model you are using. As human beings we have an in-built radar that tells us the moment someone is not quite telling the truth or where someone is putting forward a view that they do not believe in. Similarly, although we can all flex our leadership styles to some extent, we will be more comfortable with some styles than others and consequently more authentic with some than others. It is possible, with practice, to become reasonably proficient with a range of leadership styles as long as there is a degree of congruence between your own personal values/wishes and the particular leadership approach.

QUESTIONS FOR REFLECTION

1. To what extent do your values influence your behaviour as a project manager and in what way?

2. Do you always try to be honest and open with your team members and if not, under what situations do you avoid being open and honest and why?

3. To what extent do you utilise your values and what you believe in to motivate and enthuse your team?

4. Are the current projects that you are involved in congruent with your personal values?

5. What do you know about the personal values of your individual team members?

Which Leadership Style Should Project Managers Use and Why?

The simple answer to the above questions is that leadership is more of an art than a science and there is no formula that tells us which leadership style to use in which situation. The important thing, however, is that you are aware of the leadership style(s) that you are most comfortable with and recognise when it is appropriate to use that one and when you need to step out of your comfort zone and use an alternative leadership style. To take an example, from what we have seen of leadership styles so far, the more democratic, affiliative, visionary types of style are going to gain you the most 'buy-in' from your project team and stakeholders because they facilitate good relationships. The more task-focused, commanding types of leadership style are likely to be most useful when you have a crisis to deal with or perhaps where team members are not ready or capable of performing at the appropriate level.

Many of the characteristics of the emotionally intelligent leadership style are also necessary in order to be a good change manager as we will see in Chapter 9 when we go on to look at the complexities of change management. Below are some questions that you may wish to reflect on to help you consider your most and least comfortable leadership style and how you will develop yourself as a leader.

Questions for Reflection

1. What is your preferred style of leadership, that is, what style have you felt most comfortable with in the past?

2. Which style(s) of leadership have you felt most uncomfortable with in the past?

3. What development needs will you have in changing your leadership style?

4. What triggers will you use to help you know when you should change your leadership style?

5. How will you monitor when you are changing from one leadership style to another throughout the life of the project and how will you learn from that experience?

Having looked at the types of leadership styles that might be adopted by a project manager it would probably now be useful to go and look at ways in which the project manager might start to build his team and some of the techniques available to him.

3

Building the Project Team and its Culture

So far, we have looked at the skills required by a project team and the type of leadership styles that work best. In this chapter we are going to look at how to build a good project team that will give your project the best possible chance of succeeding. We will look at the roles that people habitually play within teams and look at one way of exploring how people relate to each other in teams. We will then go on to look at how to use positive psychology to help build a project team. Finally, we will go on to look at team culture and how to create an environment that facilitates high-performing teams.

The Characteristics of Teams

If you remember, in the previous chapter one of the styles of leadership that we explored, the managerial grid, was based on two dimensions, that is, task focus and people focus. Verma (1995) suggests that effective teams can also be characterised by certain task- and people-oriented characteristics:

TASK-ORIENTED

- commitment to technical success

- on schedule, on budget performance

- commitment to producing high-quality results

- innovative and creative

- flexibility and willingness to change

- ability to predict trends

PEOPLE-ORIENTED

- high involvement work interest and high energy

- capacity to solve conflicts

- good communication

- good team spirit

- mutual trust

- self-development of team members

- effective organisational interface

- high need for achievement and growth

Verma's characteristics are covered in an earlier theory proposed by Michael West (1994) where he acknowledges that lack of homogeneity across teams makes it difficult to give a precise formula that will create effective teams. This is particularly true of project teams where the composition of skills, technical expertise and level varies tremendously from one project to another. West (1994) suggests that we should look at team effectiveness in terms of three components:

1. Task effectiveness – the extent to which the team is successful in achieving its task-related objectives.

2. Mental health – refers to the well-being, growth and development of team members.

3. Team viability – is the probability that a team will continue to work together and function effectively.

A number of project teams these days tend to be virtual or include some virtual members so it is worth looking at what research into virtual teams can tell us about team effectiveness. Two researchers, Gibson and Cohen (2003), investigated the characteristics that best enabled virtual teams to function and they found the following to be important: shared understanding, integration and mutual trust. One could argue that these three factors are implicit in the West (1994) theory. Similar to the 'transformational' leadership model and 'authentic leadership', emerging research is demonstrating the increasing role that trust and integrity play in interpersonal relationships and it is worth keeping this in mind.

If we use West's theory as our basis (whilst bearing mind the importance of trust and integrity), then the process of building a project team should be concerned with helping the team to identify and focus on its objectives whilst facilitating an environment in which team members can develop and function collectively as a team. So where should the project manager start? There are many books about teams and project teams where detailed suggestions are provided with regard to identifying tasks and so on, therefore we are not going to focus on those; instead we are going to look at the second and third elements of West's theory, that is, the well-being and growth of the team and how to ensure that members function effectively as a team. In my experience, this is more important with project teams because generally speaking they have a more limited shelf-life than established work teams. They also have a less stable membership, which means that cohesiveness has to be developed on a much shorter timeframe.

Building the Project Team?

The starting point for any project manager, once the team has been appointed, is getting to know the team members as individuals and identifying their relative strengths. There are many different ways in which this could be achieved.

THE ROLES THAT PEOPLE PREFER TO PLAY IN TEAMS

Following his extensive research with management teams, Meredith Belbin (1991) concluded that the compatibility of a team is crucial to its effectiveness. He suggested that individuals habitually play certain roles in teams depending on their particular personalities and abilities. Belbin subsumed these behaviours into nine roles: Shaper, Plant, Coordinator, Monitor Evaluator, Resource Investigator, Implementer, Team Worker, Completer Finisher and Specialist. He suggested that these roles were necessary for high-performing teams and that a team could only make best use of its technical expertise when it has sufficient roles supporting teamwork functioning.

Belbin believed that these roles were essential in order to provide balance within a team. He suggested that everyone will have a role that they prefer to adopt and a secondary role that they are able to play if someone is already playing their role. Looking at the roles listed, it is not difficult to see that they would work just as well for a project team as for any other kind of team.

THE SHAPER

This role describes someone who is driven with a strong sense of achievement. This person will be the one who challenges project decisions and pushes others to deliver their responsibilities within the project plan. A project team member acting in this role will literally help 'shape' the project but is likely to be headstrong and respond emotionally in the face of disappointment or frustrations when the project is thrown off track.

THE PLANT

This role is a creative role and the team member operating in this role is likely to generate innovative ideas for the project and creative ways of solving project difficulties. The team member in this role may be slightly introverted and may react strongly to both praise and criticism.

THE COORDINATOR

This role describes someone who keeps the project team on track towards their goals. They are calm, mature and not only understand what individual team members bring to the project but also how best to harness those strengths.

THE MONITOR EVALUATOR

This role is very important when making project decisions. The team member acting in this role will be shrewd and analytical. They are usually highly critical thinkers and take their time to mull things over so that they can take account of all factors.

THE RESOURCE INVESTIGATOR

This role is about knowing what resources are available and how to find them. Team members operating in this role are likely to be good communicators both within the project team itself and with the wider group of stakeholders. They are good negotiators and skilled in identifying new opportunities.

THE IMPLEMENTER

The team member in this role will be a practical, common-sense sort of person who approaches project difficulties in a routine and systematic manner. They are not afraid to get their hands dirty and will do whatever needs to be done.

THE TEAM WORKER

This role describes the 'people' person in the project team. The team member in this role will be interpersonally sensitive and will exercise tact and diplomacy in dealings with other project team members. They will try to ensure that everyone in the team is able to make a contribution and they will provide support to other project team members.

THE COMPLETER FINISHER

The team member acting in this role will be the one that makes sure that all the 'i's are dotted and the 't's are crossed with regard to the project. This team member will have a keen eye for detail and will prefer not to delegate so that they can ensure that everything is delivered on budget and to time.

THE SPECIALIST

This team member, as the name suggests, is someone with technical expertise in their field who regards their role as maintaining professional standards in the project. The person in this role will provide in-depth technical expertise and will take pride in their ability to do this.

When looking at these roles, it is easy to see how each role would be necessary within a project team and it is important to ensure that the activities described by these roles are delivered within your team.

QUESTIONS TO REFLECT ON

1. Do you have a balanced/compatible team?

2. Are several project members operating in the same way? For example, do you have more than one person acting as the 'plant' (this can lead to conflict)?

3. Do you have any gaps in your team with regard to the roles that Belbin proposes?

4. Are you clear which of your project team members could step into a different role if there are gaps?

How People Relate to Each Other in Teams

Going back to Belbin's (1991) assertion that compatibility in teams is crucial to their effectiveness, let us go on to look at some ways in which the potential interrelationships between team members can be explored.

INDIVIDUAL CHARACTERISTICS

In this section, we look at the tools that a project manager can use to start gaining a better understanding of individual team member's preferred ways of working and the particular strengths that they can contribute to the team. We will look at the Myers Briggs Type Indicator (MBTI), Positive Psychology and Transactional Analysis (TA).

MBTI

In order to build an effective team, it is necessary to know something of the individuals that comprise the team, for example their preferred ways of doing things and their strengths. One tool that has been used extensively with teams to help them understand each other's styles and preferences has been the 'Myers Briggs Type Indicator' (MBTI). 'OPP', who market the MBTI, suggest that the MBTI is an instrument that helps people to 'appreciate important differences between people and understand how different types can work together in a complementary way'.

The MBTI is a based on the work of Swiss psychiatrist Carl Jung and uses a questionnaire to identify individual preferences. The MBTI needs to be administered by someone who is trained to use the instrument. The outcome of the questionnaire is that everyone receives a four-letter type that best describes their preferences on the following scales:

- Extraversion–Introversion

- Sensing–Intuition

- Thinking–Feeling

- Judging–Perceiving

Someone who had a high preference for 'extraversion', 'intuition', 'thinking' and 'judging' would have the type ENTJ. Each of the four-letter 'type's has certain characteristics associated with it for example, a brief description for our ENTJ would be as follows (Briggs Myers 2000):

> Frank, decisive, assumes leadership readily. Quickly see illogical and inefficient procedures and policies, develop and implement comprehensive systems to solve organisational problems. Enjoy long-term planning and goal setting. Usually well informed, well read; enjoy expanding their knowledge and passing it onto others. Forceful in presenting their ideas.

Let's have a closer look at the scales so that you can see what relevance they might have for a project team.

Table 3.1   Extraversion/Introversion

Extraversion	Introversion
Prefer to 'talk through' problems	Prefer to 'think through' problems
Learn best through doing or discussing	Learn best by reflection/mental practice
Tend to speak and act first and reflect later	Tend to reflect before acting or speaking

It is clear from the above scales that team members with preferences at either end of the spectrum will behave rather differently in team meeting situations. The team member with a preference for extraversion will probably be quite loud and vocal, whereas the team member with a preference for introversion is more likely to contribute nothing as they will be reflecting on what has been said before formulating an opinion. There is a potential danger here for project managers in that, if you are unaware of these individual differences you might do one of the following:

- you might rely on what the vocal person has said because you have no alternative viewpoints put forward

- you might infer that the quieter team members are not interested or have nothing to contribute

The likelihood of this increases when time pressures are high and you have to make decisions quickly. As a project manager, it is important to know about individual preferences and strengths so that you can ensure that your get the maximum contribution from your team.

Table 3.2   Sensing/Intuition

Sensing	Intuition
Focus on what is real and actual	Focus on 'big picture' possibilities
Value practical applications	Value imaginative insights
Factual and concrete, notice details	Abstract and theoretical
Observe and remember specifics	See patterns and meanings
Enjoy the present	Enjoy anticipating the future
Want information to be accurate and precise	Stimulated by ambiguity
Trust experience	Trust inspiration

You will notice a difference between team members at opposite ends of the scale. The team member with a preference for 'sensing' is likely to be looking very much at the facts of a situation and using his past experience to produce a solution. A team member with a preference for 'intuition' is more likely to be focusing on the future possibilities of a situation. He will not care about past experience but instead will be looking for a new and innovative way to solve the problem. Both of these ways of thinking are useful when managing projects, as there are times when it is appropriate to focus very much on hard data and concrete facts. Equally, there are sometimes during the life cycle of the project when you need someone who can be creative and visionary.

Table 3.3   Thinking/Feeling

Thinking	Feeling
Guided by objective logic	Guided by personal values and convictions
Focus on cause and effect	Focus on harmony with own and other's values
Look for flaws in logic	Look for common ground and shared values
Apply consistent principles in dealing with people	Treat each person as a unique individual
At work emphasise involvement with tasks	At work emphasise and support the process

This scale is another interesting one for project managers to consider because it gives an insight into how people like to be rewarded. People with a preference for 'thinking' like to be rewarded for the achievement of tasks, particularly where the recognition comes from someone with the expertise to understand how good a job they have done. On the other hand, people with a preference for 'feeling' like to be appreciated for who they are and the effort that they have put into something, that is, they like a more personal touch.

Table 3.4   Judging/Perceiving

Judging	Perceiving
Like to get things decided	Like to keep options open
Scheduled and organised	Spontaneous and adaptable
Enjoy decision-making and planning	Enjoy the process, no decision before its time
Dislike working under time pressure	Energised by last-minute time pressures
Like to decide as soon as is reasonable to do so	Like to keep decisions open as long as is reasonable to do so

Project managers will see a rather different approach to deadlines with people at the opposite ends of this scale. Team members with a preference for the 'judging' end of the scale will plan carefully and meticulously, taking all contingencies into account. Team members with a preference for the 'perceiving' end will still meet their deadlines but in a much more flexible and less structured way. This may cause frustrations for those team members who like to follow plans to the letter. In addition, team members with a preference for the 'perceiving' approach may become frustrated with their 'judging' colleagues who may appear a little rigid and dogmatic.

From looking at these scales it is clear that there needs to be a balance between the scales as it would probably be fairly disastrous for a project team to have everyone with the same preference; for example, what would happen if the entire team preferred not to plan? Clearly, there is room in a project team to accommodate a range of preferences but there may be occasions when you have to ask certain team members to operate from their non-preferred end of the scale.

HOW WOULD YOU USE MBTI IN A TEAM CAPACITY?

The first step, of course would be to ask your team members to complete the Myers Briggs Type Inventory, which they can do either in hard copy or online. Once all team members have identified their 'best fit' team type (for example, ENTJ) this information can be used to help the team understand each other better. Depending on the outcome of this, various exercises can be carried out with the team to promote understanding and effective team working.

The outcome of the team completing the questionnaire could be one of the following:

- The team is very diverse, that is, well balanced.

- The team is fairly homogeneous with people having very similar preferences.

- There may be a core of the team who are very similar and a small group who are different.

Obviously, the first possible outcome is a good start because it means that people can continue to use their preferred way of operating. There would still be a need, however, to help the team understand and appreciate their diversity. The second and third possible outcomes will probably require more input. If team members are too similar, you may not have the necessary blend of behaviours and this is one situation where you may have to ask certain team members to operate from their lesser preferred option; for example, if you have a project team where no one has a preference for detailed planning, you may have to ask a couple of your spontaneous team members to focus on this activity, in order to ensure that an efficient and effective project plan is produced.

The final outcome will also require some intervention, in that if you have a small group who are in the minority with regard to their preferences then you will have to ensure that exercises are carried out with the team which encourage an understanding and awareness of each other's different preferred ways of working. This will help facilitate effective team working and avoid unnecessary obstacles to communication.

QUESTIONS FOR REFLECTION

1.   Do you know which of your project team members need interaction with you or other team members in order to solve problems and which ones need time and space for personal reflection?

2.   Do you know which of your project team members can offer you a strategic view on the project and which ones a pragmatic one?

3.   Do you know which of your team members require you and their team members to share emotions and which ones need objectivity when dealing with project dilemmas and problems?

4.   Are you aware of how flexible or rigid an approach each of your project team members adopts with regard to project planning and delivery?

Positive Psychology and Project Management

In the past, psychology was very much focused on the negative aspects of the human psyche such as mental illness; however, a new branch of psychology has emerged that instead focuses on the strengths and virtues of human beings. Not surprisingly, this branch of psychology is known as 'positive psychology'. Gable and Haidt (2005) define positive psychology as 'the study of the conditions and processes that contribute to the flourishing or optimal functioning of people, groups and institutions'.

Seligman (2004) suggests that there are three strands to positive psychology, that is, the study of positive emotion, the study of positive individual traits and the study of the positive institutions, for example close families. Let's start by looking at the first strand, that is, positive emotion.

WHAT IS POSITIVE EMOTION

Positive emotions play a large role in evolution according to Fredrickson (in Seligman 2004): 'They broaden our abiding intellectual, physical and social resources, which we can draw upon whenever a threat or opportunity presents itself.' Seligman goes on to suggest that other people are more receptive towards us when we are positive which is more conducive to building good relationships (very important in project management). He also suggests that we are more open to new ideas and experiences when we are feeling positive (also important in project management). Negative emotions tend to be more restrictive in that they leave us feeling distrustful, defensive and more inward looking.

Current research suggests that we all have a 'steady state' level of happiness which is our day-to-day overall happiness level. This will increase from time to time with short bursts of extra happiness in response to positive events, for example good news. There is evidence that this enduring level of happiness can be increased through various measures, some of which could be created in a team environment. On his website (www.authentichappiness.sas.upen.edu), Seligman has a questionnaire called The 'general happiness scale' which you and your team members can complete free of charge online. This will provide you with a baseline of the enduring level of happiness that each of your team members experiences. This will give you a feel for whether you will need to put a lot of effort into boosting positivity levels or whether you will just need to work at boosting them during difficult times.

SIGNATURE STRENGTHS

Research carried out by (Seligman 2004) identified 24 strengths or virtues that he named 'signature strengths'. These signature strengths are perceived to have two characteristics: 'First, strength is a *trait*, a psychological characteristic that can be seen across different situations and over time. Second, strength is *valued in its own right*.' By this, Seligman means that these strengths often provide benefits but we value them even if they do not produce any directly observable benefits, for example being honest. Seligman found that his 24 signature strengths were found across all cultures in the world. He suggests that we all have a subset of these strengths that become our own signature strengths. He also suggests that, as human beings, we are far happier and more productive, whether in work or any other environment, if we are engaged in tasks that enable us to utilise our signature strengths. It follows, then, that if you can identify the signature strengths of your project team then you can allocate tasks in a way that utilises those strengths. This will help you create a more positive and more productive project team. There is a questionnaire on Seligman's website (mentioned earlier) called the 'Brief Strengths Test' and you and your team members can complete this free of charge online.

The signature strengths are as follows:

Table 3.5   Signature strengths

Number	Signature strength	Signature strengths
1	Curiosity/Interest in the world	This strength is about being open to new experiences
2	Love of learning	This is about learning new things because you can
3	Judgement/Critical thinking	This is about logic
4	Ingenuity/Practical intelligence	This strength is about solving problems creatively
5	Social intelligence	This is about the ability to relate to others
6	Perspective	This is about being someone that other people will seek counsel from
7	Valour and bravery	This is about having the strength of your convictions
8	Perseverance/diligence	This is about achieving what you set out to do
9	Integrity/Honesty	This is about being authentic
10	Kindness/Generosity	This is about helping others
11	Loving/Allowing oneself to be loved	This strength is about having close relationships with others
12	Citizenship/Teamwork	This strength is about being a team player
13	Fairness and equity	This strength is about doing what is right
14	Leadership	This is about being able to make things happen whilst maintaining good relationships
15	Self-control	This strength is about managing one's emotions and impulses
16	Prudence/Discretion	This strength is about avoiding knee-jerk reactions
17	Humility/Modesty	This strength is about not being boastful
18	Appreciation of beauty and excellence	This strength is about the ability to appreciate beauty per se
19	Gratitude	This strength is about the ability to thank people
20	Hope/Future mindedness	This strength is about having positive goals and working towards them
21	Spirituality/Sense of purpose	This strength is about the ability to believe in something
22	Forgiveness and mercy	This is about the ability to forgive
23	Playfulness and humour	This is about light-heartedness and making people laugh
24	Zest/Enthusiasm	This is the ability to put your all into something

Related to the theory of signature strengths is the concept of 'flow'. 'Flow' is a state of mind where an individual is so intensely engaged in an activity that their self-consciousness is emerged in it and they experience an altered sense of time (Csikszentmihalyi et al. 2005). Research has shown that 'flow' most commonly occurs when there is a high degree of challenge which stretches an individual's skill to the extreme. It is not too difficult to imagine the sorts of benefits that would be reaped from having a project team that operate in 'flow'. Linley and Harrington (2006) suggest that the identification and use of signature strengths could be one factor in helping facilitate 'flow'. Csikszentmihalyi et al. (2005) suggest that three factors contribute to the facilitation of 'flow', that is, having a clear set of goals, a balance between perceived challenge and perceived skills and clear (and immediate) feedback. These three should be familiar concepts for project managers.

There are three further aspects of positive psychology that are worth mentioning: dealing with negative events, using gratitude and using forgiveness.

DEALING WITH NEGATIVE EVENTS

Our memories from past events are tinged with emotions and when we are reminded of those past events we will feel the same emotion again, sometimes just as strongly as though we were reliving the event. Consequently, if a project team has experienced a failure or set back which has led to negative feelings then keep referring back to it in subsequent meetings will reinvigorate those same negative feelings. This could prevent people from focusing positively and productively on current tasks and it is something that project managers need to be aware of. Talking about negative events from the past is fine but you may have to have a strategy in place to lift emotions again. There are two strategies that you can use to help deal with such negative events and/or to promote good mood generally amongst the team, that is, gratitude and forgiveness.

GRATITUDE

Gratitude, as the name suggests, is about being thankful for the good things in life and research has shown that being thankful does provide a positive boost. Seligman (2004) in his research, asked participants to write testimonies about significant people in their lives (for example, mother), thanking them for everything that they had done for them. Seligman also asked participants to compile a list of five things that they felt grateful for, for example, waking up in the morning, being in good health and so on. This technique could be modified for a project team setting in that, if the project team has experienced a failure or setback, perhaps they could be asked to look for things to be grateful for regarding the situation, for example the opportunity to learn from it. Obviously this depends on the absence of a punitive culture and we will go on to look at culture later in this chapter.

FORGIVENESS

This is another concept from positive psychology and it is based on the premise that 'Frequent and intense emotions about the past are the raw material that blocks the emotions of contentment and satisfaction and these thoughts make serenity of mind impossible' (Seligman 2004). This could be used in a project team setting, perhaps where someone has been upset/angered by the action of a team member or stakeholder. The idea is that the angered/upset individual, instead of harbouring negative thoughts, forgives the perceived perpetrator. Seligman quotes a technique used by (Worthington) which uses the acronym REACH which is described as:

- *R* ecall – recall the painful event in an objective way without thinking negatively of the perpetrator

- *E* mpathise – try to understand the painful event from the perpetrator's point of view

- *A* ltruistic – give the gift of forgiveness

- *C* ommit – commit yourself publicly to forgiving this person, for example in the team setting

- *H* old onto forgiveness. Avoid dwelling on the negative memories and keep reminding yourself that you have forgiven the person.

HOW CAN POSITIVE PSYCHOLOGY HELP YOU CREATE A WINNING PROJECT TEAM?

Let us briefly summarise the techniques from positive psychology that you can utilise to improve team well-being and project delivery:

- The environment plays a part in influencing our emotions either negatively or positively. The brighter and more pleasant the environment, the more positive a mood will be created. If you need to generate creative and tolerant thinking then you need a bright and stimulating environment. A simple starting point could be ensuring that all your meetings take place in a well-lit, pleasant room.

- Do not dwell on project failures or negative experiences as this will just reinstate any associated negative emotions and will lower the mood of the project team. If an aspect of the project has not gone well, identify any learning points and then move on to more positive areas of discussion such as achievements within the project.

- Get team members to express gratitude; for example, if a team member or stakeholder has done something for them, encourage the team to acknowledge this. Gratitude increases positive feelings both in the giver and the recipient. A quick telephone call, email or personal 'thank you' provides an emotional uplift for both the giver and the recipient.

- Be aware of any pessimistic tendencies in your team and be mindful of them. Pessimists tend to give up more easily than optimists. You may have to be prepared to give more encouragement to project team members with pessimistic tendencies in order to boost their confidence and a belief that they can succeed by persevering.

- Try to keep fun alive within the team but vary the experiences because people's level of enjoyment soon habituates, that is, becomes satiated, and the quality of the experience diminishes. Keep it fresh. Research has shown that an element of surprise prevents pleasure from habituating.

- Where possible, try to ensure that you assign your project team members to tasks that best utilise their signature strengths, as they will be happier and more productive.

QUESTIONS FOR REFLECTION

1. To what extent are your project team happy and motivated to achieve?

2.   To what extent are you aware of project team member's personal strengths and the impact that they have on their enthusiasm and competence for project delivery?

3.   How often are your project team members in 'flow'?

Using Transactional Analysis to Understand How Team Members Relate to Each Other

When teams are formed, team members have to learn about each other and build good relationships. One tool which has been widely used over the years to address communication in teams is 'Transactional Analysis' (TA). The practice of Transactional Analysis was introduced initially by Eric Berne in the 50s. It is based on the work of Sigmund Freud and uses his concepts of the ego, id and superego. Good communication is important for most teams, but even more so for project teams who have to influence and engage a range of stakeholders in order to deliver projects.

Berne suggested that we interact with others from one of three states: the child (id), the adult (ego) or the parent (superego). When we communicate from the state of 'child' we tend to be impulsive and immature. The 'child' state can either be 'free child' where the individual behaves in a spontaneous way without concern for the reactions of others or 'adapted child' where the individual behaves as if a parent was watching or listening.

When we communicate from the 'adult' state we tend to be cool-headed and rational. We will use our logic and evaluate options. We will be objective. When we communicate using the 'parent' state we will either be supportive and protecting (nurturing parent) or judgemental and evaluative (critical parent). All three states are deemed necessary for a healthy personality; however, the 'adult' state is considered to be the most effective medium for interpersonal interaction.

According to TA, there are three types of transactions (or interpersonal interactions): complementary transactions, crossed transactions and ulterior transactions. Complementary transactions occur where both the communicator and the recipient utilise the same stage, for example adult to adult, child to child or parent to parent. Crossed transactions occur when the recipient responds with an incompatible ego state, for example the boss talks to an employee using the 'adult' state and says 'Mary, those reports you were completing are now two days overdue, when do you think they will be finished?' and Mary responds from the 'child' state and says 'Oh forget it! I will look for another job tomorrow.' These types of transactions tend to damage interpersonal relations. The final set of transactions, that is, ulterior transactions, are more subtle and more complicated. They tend to occur where someone portrays a certain state, for example 'adult', but actually means a different state altogether. These types of transactions can also be very damaging to interpersonal relationships.

Luthans (1989) gives the example of a boss who tells his staff that his door is always open and that they should come in and air their problems so that they can find a solution together. This is very much the 'adult' stage. What the boss really means, however, is, 'Don't come whining to me with your problems – find an answer yourself,' which is very much critical parent.

Luthans (1989) suggests that these types of transactions are the most difficult to identify and deal with.

LIFE POSITIONS

Barker (1980) proposes another way of looking at team relationships using TA and that is through concept of 'life positions. A person's 'life position' indicates how he is relating to other people at any point in time. The four life positions are indicated in Figure 3.1 which is known as the 'OK corral' (Barker 1980).

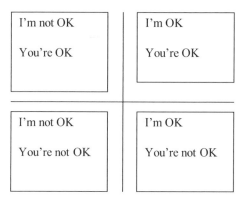

Figure 3.1   The OK corral

I'M OK, YOU'RE OK

People in this position are happy and optimistic about work. They use their time well and get on with people. They collaborate with others and are respectful of senior managers. This is known as the 'get on' position because people in this position are likely to succeed (Barker 1980).

I'M OK, YOU'RE NOT OK

This is known as the 'get rid of' position by Barker (1980) and is characterised by feelings of anger and hostility towards others. Colleagues are perceived as inferior and incompetent. An individual in this position may be highly competitive and will climb over anyone in order to achieve power and status.

I'M NOT OK, YOU'RE OK

This is known as the 'get away from' position by Barker (1980) and occurs when someone is feeling inadequate and/or powerless. People in this situation tend to constantly put themselves down. They withdraw from difficult situations and problems and generally do not achieve much success whilst in this state of mind.

I'M NOT OK, YOU'RE NOT OK

This is the 'get nowhere' position by Barker (1980) and is characterised by feelings of confusion. People in this state of mind tend to have an attitude of 'Why bother?' Needless to say, people in this state do not achieve a great deal of success.

The four states described are transitory states of mind, in that team members can be assisted to move from a negative state to a more positive state. Ideally, you need everyone in your project team to be operating from 'I'm OK, You're OK'.

TA then provides an additional tool to help team members reflect on the way in which they communicate with each other and it can be very helpful in understanding why conflict occurs, thinking about the four states discussed above.

QUESTIONS FOR REFLECTION

1.   Are you feeling OK?

2.   Do you know whether or not each of your project team members is feeling OK?

Team Culture

Culture has been defined in many ways by many different theorists; for example, 'culture is a characteristic of all organisations through which, at the same time, their individuality and uniqueness is expressed. The culture of an organisation refers to the unique configuration of norms, values, beliefs, ways of behaving and so on that characterise the manner in which groups and individuals combine to get things done ... ' (Crombie, in Furnam and Gunter 1993). Teams within organisations will generally share the overall organisational culture but they may have some slight differences. Unlike most teams, project teams are unlikely to have an existing culture because they are usually pulled together specifically to deliver a certain task or set of tasks and will probably have not worked together before. Consequently the project manager has to determine the culture of the project team. There are a number of factors that contribute to culture and by manipulation of these factors the desired culture can be achieved.

At its simplest level, organisational culture is about constituent members having shared values and shared norms about what behaviours are acceptable within the organisation. Culture is very important both to teams and organisations in that it can make a difference between being successful and not being successful. Many attempts have been made to identify the characteristics of organisational culture, for example, Schein (1993) and Hofstede (1986).

Hofstede's (1986) characteristics apply quite well to the team situation in that they suggest that there are four characteristics of culture: power distance dimension, uncertainty avoidance, individualism/collectivism and masculinity/femininity. So let's explore these categories and what they mean for a project manager.

POWER DISTANCE

As the name suggests, this category refers to the balance of power in the team and as part of the culture, the project manager will have to give this matter some consideration. For example:

- How much autonomy will you permit individual team members to have and how much control do you wish to retain personally?

- How flat a team structure will you have? Will everyone report directly to you or will you have other managers/supervisors?

- Will all roles within the team be valued equally?

- Who will be able to legitimately make decisions for the team and to what level?

- At what point will you wish to be consulted before a decision is made and will this be in regard to all decisions or just certain categories of decisions?

MASCULINITY/FEMININITY

This characteristic is really about the things which the team values and the questions that you, as project manager, will have to ask yourself about:

- What type of values do you want as the ethos for the team? do you want values around caring for people and being intuitive or values around aggression and competition?

- Do you want people's private lives to be kept totally separate from team activity or do you want the demarcation lines to be more blurred?

INDIVIDUALISM/COLLECTIVISM

This characteristic of culture is about the extent to which team members are encouraged to be self-reliant vs the extent to which they are encouraged to use each other for support. Questions you may want to ask yourself include:

- Do you want the project team to feel quite impersonal, that is, everyone gets on with their respective tasks, or do you want the team to feel more like a family?

- Do you want the project team to defend its members or would you prefer each team member to defend their own interests?

- Do you want to use practices that encourage individual initiative or practices based on loyalty and group participation?

UNCERTAINTY/AVOIDANCE

This characteristic, as the name suggests, is about the extent to which people feel threatened by ambiguity and the extent to which they avoid ambiguous situations. The areas that you will need to consider are as follows:

- Will you make all activities very structured or less so?

- Will you have any written rules and if so for which areas of work?

- Will you encourage project team members to be generalists or specialists?

- Do you want to try and control any of the variability and if so, to what degree?

- How will you encourage people to take risks and how will you support them in doing this?

Research has shown that people are more likely to take risks where they feel supported, there is a no-blame culture and they are trusted/empowered to take those risks. We will go on to look at 'risk taking' in more detail later on in the book.

Team Climate

Remember that earlier we said that 'culture' is about shared values and shared norms of behaviour. We are now going to look briefly at the 'climate' of a team or organisation. 'Climate' is the psychological atmosphere of the team or organisation. It is very important 'because of the significant relationships exhibited between this construct and job satisfaction and job performance' (Furnham and Gunter 1993). They go on to suggest that the creation of a healthy psychological climate in a team or organisation is due to leadership behaviour and style. Back in the 80s, Mullins (1989) suggested a number of factors which organisations with a healthy psychological climate would exhibit. These factors still look relevant in the twenty-first century and look as relevant for project teams as they do for other teams and organisations. Many of the elements listed below will be very familiar as we have already touched on them in previous discussions.

FACTORS THAT CREATE A GOOD PSYCHOLOGICAL CLIMATE

- the integration of organisational goals and personal goals

- a flexible structure with a network of authority, control and communications, with autonomy for individual members

- styles of leadership appropriate to particular work situations

- mutual trust, consideration and support amongst different levels of the organisation

- recognition of individual differences and attributes and of people's needs and expectations at work

- attention to job design and the quality of working life

- challenging and responsible jobs with high performance standards

- equitable systems of reward based on positive reinforcement

- opportunities for personal development, career progression and advancement

- justice in treatment and fair personnel and industrial relations policies and practices

- the open discussion of conflict with emphasis on the settlement of differences without delay or confrontation

- democratic functioning of the organisation with full opportunities for genuine consultation and participation

- a sense of identity with and loyalty to the organisation and a feeling of being needed and an important member of the organisation

TEAM PROCESSES TO AVOID

So far, we have talked about a range of individual and team attributes that would be desirable in various team situations; however, there are also pitfalls to be avoided. There are two main team processes that are unhelpful and it is probably worth briefly mentioning them so that they can be avoided. The two processes are groupthink and social loafing.

'Groupthink' is a term coined by Janis (1972). It describes a process of 'a deterioration of mental efficiency, reality testing and moral judgement that results from in-group pressures'. Basically, Janis suggests that when teams are too cohesive, the aim of every discussion is to reach consensus (and not necessarily the best option). Consequently, no real appraisal of decisions takes place and minority views are quashed (sometimes brutally) in the concern to reach consensus. In order to avoid this process, it is important to ensure that all views are aired and that minority opinions are given the same consideration as the majority ones. This is particularly true in project teams which may have not been in existence for very long or may not have had the opportunity to bond and develop naturally in the way that longer-term, co-located teams have. It is easy to imagine how a project team that engaged in 'groupthink' would be unlikely to make the best decisions for the project.

The second process to be avoided is what West (1994) refers to as 'social loafing'. This is something that occurs in teams where individual effort and contribution is not easily identified. Certain individuals do less when working in a team than they would working independently, that is, they put less effort into achieving anything because they feel that no one is any the wiser as their efforts would be hidden anyway in the overall efforts of the team. The moral here, then, is to ensure that everyone has objectives to deliver and that the delivery is measurable and attributable to someone. Once again, there is an increased potential for social loafing in project teams which are often either virtual or none co-located. In addition, project team members often have a day job to do as well and may assume that someone else within the project will pick up the slack. Obviously, social loafing has an impact on project delivery and the ability of the project team to deliver on time.

4

Coaching the Project Team

Coaching can be used in two ways with regard to teams, in that it can be utilised as a leadership style and it can also be used as a particular method for developing a team. In the previous chapter we talked about team culture and the extent to which team members are empowered to get on with their jobs. We also talked about team climate and motivating team members. Coaching as a leadership style is where the project manager uses coaching techniques during conversations and general interactions with project team members. A coaching style can be used to motivate and empower project team members as well as developing them. It also provides another method of helping to improve team performance. Coaching is relevant for individuals and teams generally but also lends itself well to project teams.

In the first part of this chapter, we will start off by looking at coaching as a leadership style and the underlying skills required for any form of coaching. We will also look at one of the most popular models to be utilised in coaching. We will then go on to look more specifically at team coaching.

When Is a Coaching Style Useful in Leadership?

Coaching styles of leadership are most relevant when you have mature followers (see Hersey and Blanchard's situational leadership model in Chapter 2) and are less useful when you have inexperienced or unskilled project team members. In these situations you are likely to need to be more directive until the individual has sufficient skill and confidence to be able to benefit from a more open-ended coaching approach. Additional factors that can influence whether or not to utilise a coaching approach include 'time and quality factors'. Where time is of the essence (which can often be the case in certain phases of a project) being directive with regard to what needs to be done is likely to be more efficient. Similarly, where quality is crucial, there may not be the flexibility to experiment and a more directive style may be more appropriate.

What is Coaching as a Leadership Style?

> *Coaching is unlocking a person's potential to maximise their own performance. It is helping them to learn rather than teaching them. (T. Gallwey)*

Coaching evolved from the world of sport and it provides a way of relating to a team member in a manner which facilities and encourages the team member to find his or her own solutions to problems. Coaching is about helping team members to explore problems and to take responsibility for their own actions. If you cast your mind back to Chapter 2 where we looked at leadership styles and Hersey and Blanchard's model of situational leadership which included telling, selling, participating and delegating, then a coaching style would be at the 'delegating' end of this spectrum. Coaching is non-directive and does not rely on formal authority relationships. This is very useful for project teams where members are often matrix managed and there is no formal management relationship between the team member and the project leader. The other benefit of this approach is that where the leader demonstrates and models coaching behaviours, those same behaviours will be adopted by project team members and become a part of the team culture.

A Coaching Model

There are many different coaching models in existence depending on the knowledge and sophistication of the coach; however, a good one to start with is the one that is most commonly cited, that is, the 'GROW' model. This is a model quoted by John Whitmore. It is an easy model to use and ideal for anyone who is new or relatively inexperienced in the field of coaching.

THE 'GROW' MODEL

G oal-setting for the discussion as well as short-term and long-term

R eality-checking to explore the current situation

O ptions and alternative strategies or courses of action

W hat is to be done, WHEN, by WHOM, and the WILL to do it

GOAL-SETTING

In a standard coaching situation, the coachee (person being coached) will set the agenda for the meeting and will arrive with one or several issues that he wishes to explore. In a project management situation, however, there may be occasions when the project manager is the person who brings issues for discussion to the coaching session because there are things that he needs to raise. Regardless of who has actually brought the issues to the session, the purpose of this stage in the model is to establish a goal or series of goals as outcomes for the coaching session. To take an example, the project manager may have concerns that a team member is not building sufficiently good relationships with relevant stakeholders and he may have a coaching session with that team member to explore ways in which they could be more effective at this.

Useful questions at this stage might be:

- How do you feel about the relationship that you have with stakeholders?

- Are there ways in which you could further improve your relationship with stakeholders?

REALITY

This stage of the GROW model is about clarifying the current situation and being realistic about what can be achieved. The key to examining reality is to be objective. We all have slightly distorted views of ourselves and our abilities and on occasions we can be unrealistic. Self-awareness is important here in recognising one's own personal distortions in order to see things as they really are. To achieve reality then the potential distortions of both the project manager/coach and the coachee/project team member need to be addressed. The project manager/coach can help achieve this by asking questions that elicit factual answers; for example, 'What were the factors that influenced your decision?' It is important for the project manager/coach to avoid being judgemental as this is likely to lead to a defensive reaction on behalf of the project team member/ coachee.

The session will be more productive if the project manager/coach is specific and descriptive in his choice of language, as this will sound less critical. To take an example from John Whitmore (2004), he comments that you 'don't just tell a marksman that he missed – that will only make him feel bad. He wants to know that his shot was three centimetres about the bull and one and a half to the right, if he is to make the correction'. One reality question that nearly always adds value is 'What actions have to be taken so far with this?' This question is usually followed by 'What were the effects of that action?'

OPTIONS

The purpose of the options stage is not to find the right answer but to create and list as many alternative courses of action as possible. The generation of ideas is often constrained by the implicit assumptions that we carry; for example, that it can't be done, they would never agree to it, it's bound to cost too much, and so on. A good coach would encourage the client to ask themselves 'What if?' This process temporarily sidesteps the rational mind and encourages a more creative approach. 'What if?' questions could include:

- What if it was approved by the project board?

- What if stakeholders did agree?

- What if we did have the budget/resources?

WHAT

The final phase of 'What will you do?' is to convert a discussion into a decision. It involves creating an action plan to address issues that have been identified and explored during your coaching session. Useful questions at this stage might be:

- What are you going to do?

- When are you going to do it?

- What obstacles might you encounter?

- Who needs to know?

- What support do you need?

- How and when are you going to get that support?

- What other considerations do you have?

QUALITIES OF A GOOD COACH/MANAGER

There are a few qualities that tend to differentiate those managers who can coach effectively and those who cannot. Generally speaking, good coaches are:

patient	detached
supportive	interested
good listeners	perceptive
aware	self-aware
attentive	retentive

It is important to recognise that these qualities are not necessarily the ones that are normally associated with project managers and that these may be skill areas that you have to work on in order to strengthen your overall skill repertoire and ability to deliver projects effectively and on time.

Essential Coaching Skills

Adopting a coaching approach to a project team involves having a coaching philosophy and some basic coaching skills. The coaching philosophy is concerned with a belief in the capability of others. That fact that our beliefs about the capability of others has an impact on their performance has been demonstrated in a number of experiments. Studies from the field of education have demonstrated that where teachers are informed that a student is a good, adequate or poor performer has an impact on the type of grade that they receive, with those described as poor performers achieving low grades. This is also true of team members and managers. This means that in order to successfully carry out coaching we have to adopt a far more optimistic view than usual of the dormant capability of people. There are two basic skills that are needed in order to use coaching models effectively and they are 'active listening' and 'reflection'.

ACTIVE LISTENING

We all assume that 'listening' is something that we all do automatically and that is the end of it. It may surprise you, however, to know that there are different types of listening that we habitually engage in and some types are more helpful than others. There are basically three types of listening: peripheral, apparent and active.

Peripheral listening

This is the most superficial level and this type of listening simply registers the sound waves of another person's voice. You can hear someone talk and be thinking of something else or even doing something else. You do not have to pay attention to them. You should never be at this stage when attempting to use a coaching approach.

Apparent listening

This is the type of listening that we all tend to engage in on a day-to-day basis. It describes the situation where we look as though we are listening. We nod in all the right places but in reality we are thinking about what we are going to do that evening or whether we should go to Greece or Spain for our summer holiday. Once again, this type of listening is not very helpful when we are trying to create a more coaching type discussion.

Active listening

This is the type of listening that we should be utilising more if we are serious about understanding the needs and requirements of other people. This type of listening is where we really concentrate on what the other person is saying and try to understand their perspective on the situation under discussion. It is easy to see how a project manager is likely to gain a better understanding of the team member or stakeholder by using this type of listening. The concept of 'active listening' sounds deceptively simple, but unfortunately we use it far less than you would imagine. It is necessary to make a conscious effort to keep yourself focused on what the speaker is saying and avoid drifting off into other thoughts. Try it for yourself in your next one-to-one meeting with someone and see whether you can retain your concentration.

There is another level of listening that is sometimes referred to in coaching circles and that is 'conscious listening'. This is an even deeper type of listening where you try and suspend judgement and your own personal thoughts and prejudices and just concentrate solely on the speaker. There is a minimum of internal dialogue in this type of listening so that your intuition can work best. Generally speaking, with regard to the level of coaching that you are likely to utilise as a project manager, 'active listening' will be sufficient to get the results that you need.

If we searched our souls, I am sure that we could produce many reasons as to why we do not always actively listen to people; however, the main culprits that prevent us from doing this are listed below.

THE THREE ENEMIES OF ACTIVE LISTENING

Internal dialogue, that is, the running commentary that we tend to have with ourselves

When you are listening to yourself you cannot be listening to the speaker. Your internal dialogue may not be about the speaker or what they are saying, but about something completely different; for example, what time should I go to the gym tonight?

Muscle tension

It is difficult to listen when you are tense. So, if you find your attention wandering, relax. Make sure that you are comfortable. Physical discomfort is a great distracter.

A focused stare

Your mind will be more open and receptive if you use your whole visual field, so soften the focus of your eyes and widen your vision. Take in as much as you can with a soft open focus.

REFLECTION

Personal reflection is a popular tool in coaching even though it is not exclusive to coaching. It is a useful tool for project managers and general managers alike as it allows us to learn from our experiences and consequently improve how we do things.

WHAT IS REFLECTION?

Reflection is simply the process of looking back on a situation and evaluating it. The sorts of questions that we should be asking ourselves are:

- How did it go?

- Which elements worked well?

- Which elements worked less well or did not work at all?

- Which behaviours of mine were effective?

- What could I do differently?

Personal reflection is not rocket science but how often do we make the time to sit and reflect on our actions? Often it is only when something goes catastrophically wrong that we take the time to reflect. Personal reflection, however, is a very powerful tool, in terms of improving our performance and that of others. It is a good skill to acquire and a useful one to recommend to project team members.

What Is Team Coaching?

Team coaching can have two aspects. Firstly, similar to individual coaching, it can be used to help the individuals within the team to develop. The second aspect is that team coaching can be used to develop the team as an entity and increase its overall capability to act effectively and autonomously in solving its own problems.

WHY IS COACHING RELEVANT TO PROJECT TEAMS?

Coaching has a role to play not only in developing people and teams but also in helping them to get on well together and this is particularly important in temporary and/or virtual teams where it is more difficult for these processes to occur naturally as they can do in more established, mature teams.

Project managers, as with other types of managers, have a particular task or set of tasks to achieve and, as we discussed during the chapter on leadership skills, it is possible for managers to focus purely on the task at the expense of the individuals within the team and the team itself. In some ways, team coaching allows a project manager to kill two birds with one stone in that coaching the team can focus on a task that the team has not dealt particularly well with, but at the same time it can focus on the individuals that form the team. This is possible through a joint focus on team tasks and team processes. Although the name of 'team coaching' is relatively new, the dual focus on task and process is something that was very much in evidence during the sixties where lots of work was carried into group dynamics.

TEAM PROCESSES

So what do we mean when we talk about the team 'process'? The team process is the set of interpersonal interactions that accompany or underlie any team action, such as trying to solve a problem or make a decision. The function of team coaching is to facilitate group cohesion and minimise any unnecessary or unhelpful conflict. A cursory glance at the literature around small group dynamics and working with small groups emphasises the need for cohesion in any successful group or team. I don't think that any of us would argue with this point, in that most of us at some time in our lives have experienced the negative vibes associated with being part of a divided group or a group 'in conflict'. Equally, I think we would all agree that these latter two types of groups are not particularly productive.

QUESTIONS FOR REFLECTION

1. Would a coaching approach to leadership be beneficial for your project team?

2. Are your project team members experienced and mature?

3.   Do you have the time to adopt a coaching approach within project timescales or do you need something faster or more direct at this time?

4.   Do you have the skills and confidence to coach project team members?

Inclusion, Openness and Control

A psychologist called Schutz (1994) carried out research into group behaviour and on the basis of this he suggested that human beings have three basic needs with regard to their interaction with other human beings. He called these three needs 'inclusion', 'control' and 'openness'.

INCLUSION

'Inclusion' actually refers to two aspects of a human need, that is, the need to include others in our activities (that is, the need to give to others/share with others) and the need to be included in the activities of others (that is, the need to belong). The extent to which an individual includes others or wishes to be included in the activities of others varies from one individual to another and with different groups at different times. When people are thrown together in a work context such as a project team, they will take time to find out various things about each other – for example, how emotionally warm or cold someone is, how much contact they like with other people, are they constantly seeking out team members to talk to or do they tend to sit at their desk and keep their head down? On the basis of this, we come to recognise how much of a match there is between our needs (in terms of both giving and taking) and the needs of the other individuals in the group. Obviously, the extent to which there is a good match will differ and, generally speaking, the stronger the match between needs then the more positive and strong the relationship will be. Schutz developed a series of questionnaires to measure openness, control and inclusion, for example Firo B.

Team coaching can help team members to recognise their differing needs and understand each other better. Whitmore (2004) suggests that team coaching is about increasing individual and collective awareness and responsibility.

CONTROL

Control is about how much responsibility an individual wants. It is about the extent to which an individual is willing to resolve issues and make decisions. Obviously if a project team is to be successful it needs to have effective mechanisms for making decisions and resolving emerging difficulties. Team coaching can be instrumental in helping the team to recognise the individual strengths that team members bring to the team. These strengths can be called upon when a problem needs solving or information/expertise is required in order to make a decision. Team coaching can also help build team confidence in its decision-making processes. The project manager/coach will need to empower the team to take responsibility for its actions. The advantage of this is that the team will then be more able to operate autonomously thus freeing up the project manager's time to enable him to take a more strategic view whilst trusting that the team will make the appropriate decision when required. Obviously, there will be times when the project manager wants to be (and needs to be) involved in decision-making, for example where a major stakeholder is likely to be disappointed; however, this should be the exception rather than the norm.

OPENNESS OR TRUST

This is the final human need that Schutz identified and it is about our willingness to open up to others, that is, the extent to which we trust people enough to share our more personal information – for example, what we did at the weekend. We all differ in the extent to which we like to get close to people and open up to them and we differ in terms of the extent to which we want to get close to work colleagues. It is not essential that team members be the best of buddies and socialise with each other; however, there does need to be a degree of openness and sharing in order to achieve a level of cohesion. It stands to reason that the more open and trusting team members are with each other, the more confidence they will have in each other and the more cohesive they will be. Team coaching can help with this as it can facilitate a trusting environment where team members are actively encouraged to share with each other. The project manager/coach will have to accept that some people are less inclined to be open than others; however, as long as team members are aware that some members do not like to share certain types of information, they will not feel rejected and hurt which should avoid some of the friction that can occur in teams.

The 'GROW' model that we looked at earlier has been proven to work successfully with teams and with individuals and it can be used to focus on the team processes that we have just looked at.

Coaching Stakeholders

In the next chapter we will be looking at engaging stakeholders and this is another area where you can put a more 'coaching' approach into use. The techniques that we have discussed in this chapter would work equally well as a way of gaining a better understanding of your stakeholders and their requirements.

5

Engaging Stakeholders

Stakeholder Analysis

Projects have a variety of stakeholders and during the project planning phase (that is, prior to implementation) it is imperative that a stakeholder analysis is carried out in order to identify the project stakeholders and their potential impact on the project. This is important even in the smallest of projects. Getting stakeholders on-side and keeping them both on-track and on-side is crucial to the success of your project and the project manager will need to devote considerable effort to managing the stakeholders effectively. The output from the stakeholder analysis informs the project manager as to which category stakeholders fall into, that is, primary, secondary, tertiary and key stakeholders. Primary stakeholders are those who will be most affected by the project. Secondary stakeholders are those who are affected to a lesser degree and tertiary stakeholders are those for whom there will be minimum impact. The most important stakeholders, however, are the key stakeholders as they can significantly influence the success of the project and/or are very important to the project.

A good stakeholder analysis provides the project manager with information about the interests (and any conflicting interests) of stakeholders. It will also help stakeholders understand more about the project. Ultimately, it will help the project manager to identify project risks and provide a basis for negotiation. There are many articles on stakeholder analysis so there is no need to go into detailed models here. Instead, I would rather focus on the more interpersonal skills needed to successfully engage stakeholders.

Table 5.1 provides an example of one of the tools that you can use to help you with your stakeholder analysis.

Table 5.1 **A sample interest/influences grid for a project to implement electronic HR services**

High/Low power	Low interest	High interest
High power	Keep satisfied: Chief executive The senior team	Manage closely: Finance manager HR manager Trade unions IT manager
Low power	Monitor: Business customers (if the electronic HR holiday booking system fails, it could have an impact on customers, e.g. if all the staff in an office were on holiday at the same time)	Keep informed: Managers HR staff Employees

Engaging Stakeholders

Once you have identified who your stakeholders are then you will need to open a discussion with them to elicit their views towards the project and to check that they understand what the project is trying to achieve and how they can assist you in ensuring its success. This is the start of the engagement process.

WHAT DO WE MEAN BY ENGAGEMENT?

The concept of employee engagement emerged from the research into organisational commitment and organisational citizenship. Both these areas of research concerned themselves with the extent to which the individual feels part of the organisation and the extent to which his behaviours are aligned with the goals and objectives of the organisation. The relatively newer research into employee engagement has much in common with earlier research into organisational commitment and citizenship; however, the two factors that differentiate employee engagement from its predecessors are the fact that it emphasises a two-way relationship and its expectation that engaged employees will have a degree of business awareness.

The Institute for Employment Studies (IES) defines engagement as 'a positive attitude held by the employee towards the organisation and its values. An engaged employee is aware of the business context and works with colleagues to improve performance within the job for the benefit of the organisation. The organisation must work to nurture, maintain and grow engagement which requires a two way relationship between employer and employee' (IES 2004). Engagement has been found to correlate with higher performance and business improvement. Engaged individuals believe in their organisation and want to make it better. More importantly, they are willing to go the extra mile to ensure the success of their organisation. So what does this have to do with stakeholders, I can hear you say? Remember that most, if not all stakeholders, will have a day job which is likely to take up most of their time and energies so you are going to have to find some way to convince them to invest time and energy in your project. The most effective way to do this is to get them engaged in your project.

HOW TO ENGAGE STAKEHOLDERS IN YOUR PROJECT

There are a number of key criteria that have emerged from the research into engagement as being the key drivers for engagement and basically they are as follows:

- *A sense of feeling valued and involved.* Stakeholders will vary in the extent to which they personally need to feel valued and involved and as you start engaging with stakeholders, you will get a feel for which ones need the most effort. A word of caution here, though: do not forget the quiet and undemanding stakeholders as they can still scupper your project. Equally, silence on their part could indicate a polite (or impolite) lack of interest in your project, which would suggest that you need to invest more time in them and not less.

- *Being involved in decision-making.* Once again, stakeholders will vary in the extent to which they want to be involved in decision-making; however, the key to success is to make sure that stakeholders have the option of being involved. You will need to encourage them to want to be involved as this is all part of the engagement process.

- *Having the freedom to voice ideas* and knowing that those above will listen. I guess that for project managers this translates into being able to comment on the project and knowing that the project manager will take the comments seriously. This sounds like common sense but, if it is, why do so many projects get delivered that fail to meet the needs of stakeholders?

- *Feeling enabled to perform well.* This is about the project manager ensuring, where possible, that stakeholders are not only clear about what the project requires of them (and we will go on to look at Goal-Setting shortly) but that they also have the information and resources they need. The assumption is often made that stakeholders have the necessary resources available to deliver project requirements; however, this is not always the case and part of your stakeholder-engagement role will be about ensuring that they either have the appropriate resource or can acquire it (possibly with your support).

So if the above four factors are the key to making someone feel engaged, then the trick is for project managers to ensure that their stakeholders feel 'all of the above' with regard to the project. In order to make these things happen, the project manager is going to have to practise some key behaviours in his interactions with stakeholders:

- relationship-building

- honesty and openness

- building shared ownership

- building understanding

'Relationship-building' is about taking the time to start building a good relationship with stakeholders. Too many project managers operate at a transactional level where they only communicate with stakeholders when they actually want something from them or, worse still, solely through 'highlight reports'. The key is to build harmonious relationships where the stakeholder feels valued and nurtured. This does not just mean having regular contact with your stakeholder and we will go on to look at communication in Chapter 6.

Making your stakeholders feel valued and involved is about finding out about their needs and objectives and sharing your aspirations with them. This ensures that you understand what they are trying to achieve both generally and from the project. This is not just a formal exercise of asking what their objectives are and then comparing them with the project specification. This is about putting in place the building blocks of a relationship which you can then maintain as time progresses. You need to invest time in demonstrating a genuine interest not only in their work but how they *feel* about their work and the project. This will provide you with a better understanding of what really motivates them. Tell them how you feel about the project that you are trying to deliver. Be enthusiastic. Remember, when we looked at emotionally intelligent leadership in Chapter 2, we emphasised the fact that emotions transfer to those around us so if you are enthused about your project, some of that will rub off on your stakeholders. Ask their opinions on the project aims and objectives and ensure that you give their suggestions proper consideration, regardless of whether you are able to take them on board or not. We will go on to look at some helpful questions that you can use, when we look at coaching stakeholders.

'*Honesty and openness*' are crucial to building a good relationship and it is important to share news, warts and all. As human beings, we can have a tendency to shy away from bad news or play it down. This is not constructive in the long term, particularly with projects. It is better to be open about any negative aspects of the project and to work with the stakeholder to identify any ways of mitigating potential downsides. The same goes for helpful suggestions that stakeholders make regarding your project. If you have no intention of taking the suggestions on board, don't just ignore the suggestions (remember that you are trying to make stakeholders feel engaged and involved); provide the stakeholder with feedback (preferably face-to-face if possible) as to why you do not feel that his suggestions will work in the context of your project. This provides you with a further opportunity to engage the stakeholder and get their buy-in because you can ask them for any additional suggestions that they may have which will overcome the problems that their original suggestion created. This will help the stakeholder to feel that they are involved in the project and its decision-making. In addition, it will make the stakeholder feel valued because you are actively seeking their views. Remember that in Chapter 2 we talked about 'authentic leadership'? If you are providing feedback to a stakeholder they will quickly identify any discrepancy between the content of what you say and the way in which you say it, which means they will probably guess if you are simply feeding them a line.

BUILDING SHARED OWNERSHIP

The three skills that we have already looked at are all very closely connected both to each other and to 'building shared ownership', which means that there are some overlaps. Basically, building shared ownership is about using the information that you gather when building the relationship with your stakeholder to identify any common goals or aspirations around the project so that you have common ground. The next stage is to agree jointly on a way forward so that your stakeholder has as much invested in the goal as you do. The skills that we have looked at so far represent the softer skills involved in engaging stakeholders. There are, however, additional methods that you can use to engage your stakeholders. One of these methods is 'Goal-Setting Techniques'.

Agreeing Project Tasks with Goal-Setting Techniques

Goal-setting techniques can be used to facilitate clear expectations amongst stakeholders with regard to what the project requires of them. This can be used as part of the engagement process as research has shown that clarity of expectations has an impact on the degree of engagement that an individual feels towards his work/organisation.

WHAT IS GOAL-SETTING THEORY?

Goal-setting (Locke and Latham 1990) is a theory that emerged from research into work motivation. This theory was the forerunner of 'managing by objectives' and it proposes that we all work better and more efficiently when we have goals to aim for. I don't think anyone would argue with that but the theory goes a little further and proposes certain characteristics that can increase the likelihood of goals being achieved. Goals are all well and good but they have to be achievable. Locke and Latham (1978) suggest that 'Focusing on the end goal all the time would be disruptive because it would distract the individual from taking the actions needed to reach it.' Consequently, it is proposed that goals are broken down into manageable and sensible chunks. This is a crucial element for project management in order to produce a project plan.

As human beings we cope better with chunks of task that we can complete in the active pursuit of our wider goals. We are motivated by achieving goals. Project management needs to utilise this human need and ensure that large tasks are broke down into agreed chunks for different people to deliver. This action of breaking tasks down into manageable chunks (which should be completed in conjunction with key/primary (and possibly some secondary) stakeholders) will help clarify exactly what has to be delivered, when and by whom. The advantage of involving stakeholders in breaking down tasks is that apart from being able to take advantage of their business knowledge the actual act of participation in the process will increase their sense of ownership of the project and their own goals in particular.

Research has also shown that feedback is useful in helping people achieve their goals and you can develop communication mechanisms that help people recognise where they are with regard to delivering their goals and how this is impacting on other aspects of the project. Remember that stakeholders are part of your wider team and you will need to recognise and reward 'good' behaviours, that is, behaviours that drive the project forward or prevent it from slipping back. There are various ways in which you can do this depending on the size of the organisation and project, for example, by taking the trouble to make contact with someone and say 'thank you' or by giving someone a special mention in your project reports.

Positive Negotiation with Stakeholders

In an ideal world, stakeholders would always be in total agreement with what the project manager thinks should happen. Unfortunately, in real life, this is not always the case and project managers often find themselves in the situation where they have to negotiate for what they want. Negotiation involves a particular set of skills and it is an area that has been well researched over many decades. Negotiation can be described as 'a process of communication by which two or more parties reach an agreement of some description'.

We all negotiate in our everyday lives without even realising it; for example, we negotiate with our partners over whether to watch the football or a good film. We negotiate with our children regarding what time they will go to bed and what time they have to come in at night. We tend to carry out these negotiations on autopilot and we may not even be consciously aware of the strategies that we are using. We will, however, be using strategies and by becoming aware not only of the strategies that we currently use but also the alternative strategies that exist, we can improve our overall ability to successfully negotiate in all walks of life and perhaps, more importantly, with our stakeholders.

The older literature on negotiation is grounded very much in the 'bargaining' types of negotiation that used to occur between management and the trade unions back in the 70s. This approach tended to focus on positional negotiation, resistance points and compromise. It may still have its uses on occasions; however, approaches towards negotiation have moved on from this approach. Positional negotiation is something that we will all probably be familiar with. This is the approach where each party in a negotiation adopts a position and tries to maintain it. For example, the trade union may retain a stance of wanting a 5 per cent cost of living increase for their members (which is their position) and the management may maintain the position that they can afford a rise of only 3 per cent. The ensuing negotiation process would be about reaching a compromise, that is, who would move their position the most.

The art of 'principled negotiation' arose from the 'Harvard Negotiation Project' (Fisher and Ury 1991) and has now taken over from position negotiation and I think that it lends itself better to the type of negotiation tasks that project managers are likely to engage in. 'Principled negotiation' is defined by four points:

1. *Separate the person from the problem* – we human beings can become very defensive when we feel that someone is attacking an idea or objective of ours and we can start to take things personally and feel that we are being attacked personally. This is extremely unhelpful in any type of negotiation because our egos become involved and anger levels can increase. The trick is to separate the problem from the person and jointly focus on the problem and how to resolve it. Concentrate on maintaining good relations with the stakeholder(s) and emphasise a collective approach by frequent use of the word 'We'; for example, how can we resolve this problem? How should we determine which course of action is most likely to deliver the project outcomes?

2. *Focus on interests not positions* – this point harks back to something we discussed earlier when we were looking at how to engage stakeholders. We talked about spending time trying to understand what they really wanted to achieve. Stakeholders are more likely to want to understand where you are coming from if you have demonstrated a genuine interest in their requirements. This point suggests that you look beyond the stakeholders stated position; for example, 'I can't implement self-service HR in my department' to what the underlying goal is which could be not to have to make three valued administrators redundant. Once you identify exactly what the stakeholder is trying to achieve it is then easier to move away from each party's stated position and to start thinking about sensible alternatives that meet the needs of both (all) parties.

3. *Generate a variety of possibilities before deciding what to do* – negotiations can sometimes feel a little fraught and the tension has an inhibiting effect on creativity. It is more effective to take time to look at options which can bring about mutual gain (a win/win approach we will go on to look at shortly) which could result in a new set of possible approaches. Try to avoid being judgemental or too evaluative at this stage as this can inhibit creativity. The most creative solutions can sometimes emerge from an idea that initially appears to be totally off the wall. Rather than thinking 'that won't work', which is judgemental, ask yourself instead:

   – What would be the benefits of implementing that idea?
   – What would the disadvantages be?
   – What might prevent us from implementing this idea?
   – How could we overcome these obstacles?

4. *Insist that the results be based on some objective criteria* – this is more logical than picking a solution at random or one party feeling pressured into accepting a course of action. To take an example, if you and the stakeholder(s) have produced several options for the project plan, don't negotiate over which one is best; use hard evidence to be guided to the optimum decision. Any decision reached should meet established levels of quality and standards. It must also be acceptable to the people who have to implement it.

Openness and honesty are very important to an effective negotiation process and if the project manager has invested time in building good relationships based on an open, honest approach, this will make any subsequent negotiation process far easier.

Win/Win or a Zero Sum Gain

We all tend to use phrases like 'it's a win/win situation' and when it comes to negotiation it is always better to start off with this philosophy. The phrase 'win/win' comes from 'game theory' which is a mathematical method of decision-making. Within 'game theory' there are three possible outcomes: the 'win/win' outcome which we are all so familiar with, the 'zero/zero' outcome where nobody wins and the 'zero sum' outcome where one person gains at another's expense. Traditional bargaining type negotiation could be deemed a 'zero sum' situation in that the object was for one party to gain a larger share of something than the other and if you imagine that the 'something' is a pot of money, it stands to reason that for one person to have more money, the other one must have less. It goes without saying that the 'zero/zero' situation where both parties lose is definitely something to be avoided when negotiating.

Project managers should always enter into negotiations with the 'win/win' philosophy fixed firmly in their minds. The advantage of this approach is that it focuses the negotiation process on creating value, 'that is, to find a way for all parties to meet their objectives, either by identifying more resources or finding unique ways to share and coordinate the use of existing resources' (Lewicki, Barry and Saunders, 2007). Lewicki et al. also suggest a few questions that a project manager can ask himself in order to prepare for a win/win outcome:

- How can both parties get what they want?

- Is there a resource shortage?

- How can resources be expanded/flexed to meet the needs of both sides?

- What issues are of higher/lower priority to me?

- What issues are of higher/lower priority to the stakeholder?

- Are there any issues that are higher/lower priority for me that are higher/lower priority for the stakeholder?

- What are the stakeholder's values and goals?

- What could I do that would make the stakeholder happy but also further progress my requirements?

- What risks and costs do my suggestions create for the stakeholder?

- What are the stakeholder's real underlying interests and needs?

- What are my own underlying interests and needs?

- Can we produce a solution that meets both sets of underlying needs and interests?

Avoid Cognitive Pitfalls

Lewicki, Barry and Saunders (2007) suggest that when we process information during a negotiation process we can be prone to certain distortions or errors in our thinking. They suggest the following thinking errors can take place: irrational escalation of commitment, mythical fixed-pie beliefs, anchoring and adjustment, availability of information and overconfidence.

- *Irrational escalation of commitment* – this is the thinking error where we can become so wedded to our cause that we continue supporting it even though it is doomed to failure, for example, arguing for a particular course of action in a project which has little chance of being successful because there are insurmountable obstacles.

- *Mythical fixed-pie beliefs* – this thinking effort supposes that there is a fixed-pie and that they have to win at the expense of the other. This is the win/lose, zero sum option that we looked at earlier under game theory. It facilitates a competitive rather than collaborative approach to negotiation and suppresses creativity.

- *Anchoring and adjustment* – this is where one party in the negotiation process sets a standard and everyone assumes that this is what that they have to negotiate around. Lewicki et al. (2007) use the example of estate agents who fix a selling price for a house and then everyone assumes this is a valid figure and negotiates around it. In other words, if you are presented with a standard of some sort during a negotiation process, check how your stakeholder arrived at that standard. It may not be a valid one.

- *Availability of information* – this is an interesting cognitive bias in that it suggests that, during a negotiation process, we remember best the information that attracts our attention such as colourful graphs and so on. This suggests that if you want a stakeholder to buy into your ideas, you will increase your chances of success if you present your argument in a colourful, easy-to-read chart such as a pie chart as opposed to a long report (Lewicki et al. 2007).

- *Overconfidence* – this is where the project manager or stakeholder believes that his ability to be right is greater than it actually is. This can lead to comments from other parties in the negotiation being ignored or devalued. Lewicki et al. (2007) describe an interesting study that was carried out which showed that negotiators who were unaware of this cognitive bias tended to overestimate their chances of success in a negotiation process and were significantly less likely to reach a compromise than negotiators who had been trained to watch out for this cognitive bias. This is food for thought, isn't it?

CREATING A POSITIVE MOOD FOR NEGOTIATION

Research has indicated that positive emotions have a positive impact on the negotiation process which is hardly surprising if you think back to Chapter 2 when we talked about emotional intelligence and the fact that our emotions can transfer to those around us. This suggests then that project managers need to find ways of raising their mood and feeling positive before entering into negotiations with stakeholders. It is also worth thinking about how you are going to remain positive throughout the negotiation process, particularly if it does not go as well as you had hoped. Regardless of how positive you are feeling about the negotiation process, do ensure that you robustly examine all arguments to ensure that you reach the best decision possible.

Coaching Stakeholders to Reach a Deeper Level of Understanding

The use of some basic coaching skills will help you to build and maintain a good relationship with your stakeholders both within and outside the negotiation process. These same skills can also be used to good effect with your project team. In particular, the use of 'Active Listening' and 'Reflection' will help you gain a better understanding of your stakeholders and their requirements. These skills are covered in Chapter 4, where we explored 'Coaching' skills.

Questions for Reflection

1. Do you have a clear strategy for engaging the project stakeholders?

2.   Are you confident that you have the skills to successfully engage stakeholders?

3.   What part do you envisage for your project team in engaging stakeholders?

4.   Are you confident that your project team members have the appropriate skills for engaging stakeholders?

5.   How will you ensure that you do not fall prey to cognitive pitfalls?

6

The People Side of Communication

In the introductory section, we talked about the factors that contribute to the failure of a large number of projects. One of these factors was communication and it is crucial that sufficient project manager time is continuously dedicated to this vital element of project management.

There are lots of materials and various resources out there which provide practical guidance on how to produce a communication plan and carry out communication within a project environment so there is no need to duplicate that. Instead we will talk about some of the underlying factors that need to be taken into account when producing the communication strategy for your project.

Understanding What Your Stakeholders Want to Know

When producing a communication plan for a project, it is very easy to think in terms of highlight reports which list the key achievements against the project plan but is this what your stakeholders want to know? Is this enough to keep them both interested and engaged in your project? Reports provide a useful tool to maintain stakeholder engagement but in order to do this you will need to provide more than a standard project highlight report. You will need to provide more customised reports that not only report on the progress of the project but specifically focus on the implications/priorities for each stakeholder; for example, rather than simply reporting that 90 per cent of project tasks have been completed to time and budget, why not make it more personal by thanking the stakeholder for any efforts that they have made in support of your project and explaining any implications that achievement or non-achievement of project tasks will have on them? Far too many projects simply rely on highlight reports and updated project plans as sole methods of communication; however, these methods alone are unlikely to engage anyone.

Understanding When and How Frequently Your Stakeholders Want to Be Informed about Project Progress

Most of the projects that I have observed tend to have a communication plan which identifies the frequency with which certain communications/reports are delivered, and the better ones are based on discussions that took place during the stakeholder analysis. This means that rather than the project team deciding on the frequency of communication, the frequency is based on the discussion held with the stakeholder during the initial stakeholder analysis and project planning phase.

Understanding Their Preferred Communication Technologies

Projects tend to vary in the communication technologies that they employ, with the larger projects using a wider variety of technologies, as you would expect. There are many more kinds of communication technology available now than ever before and it is useful to question yourself as a project manager to make sure that you are using the best technologies and not just the easiest or the ones that you are most familiar/comfortable with. Some of the available technologies include:

- email

- intranets

- internet

- virtual project offices

- webinars

- chat rooms

- face-to-face meetings

- telephone

- Skype

- conventional mail

- internal mail

Whilst producing your project plan it is important to consider the preferences of your various stakeholders with regard to the type of communication technology that you use. Different stakeholders will have differing levels of technical knowledge and some communication technologies will be easier (and more pleasant) for them to access than others. If you want to keep your stakeholders interested and engaged, it is worth ensuring that you communicate with them about the project using a means that they will actually want to use; for example, if you invite people to attend webinars and they have no idea what one is or how to join then they will probably just not attend and potentially become disenfranchised. The old adage about using the 'personal touch' can never be underestimated when it comes to getting and keeping people on board.

When feeling under pressure we are all tempted to go for the quickest and easiest method of communication but, where possible, it is always worth going for the most effective option (thinking about communication in its widest sense as opposed to just getting a message across) and considering what is likely to have the most impact, a 2-second email or a 5-minute person-to-person chat on the telephone. Face-to-face communication allows you to have a greater impact on others and provides you with an opportunity to manage that impact. Later on in this chapter we will look at some of the softer aspects of communication.

Communication planning is an essential activity for any project manager and should not be a one-off activity that results in a communication plan which is then delivered to the letter in a mechanical fashion. Communication planning is a crucial project activity and should be viewed as a continuous process which is amended strategically as the project progresses to ensure that your communication has optimum impact. In other words, your communication plan needs to go beyond the mechanics of the plan itself and act as an engagement plan.

Communication then can be a planning exercise which clearly identifies whom you will communicate with, the frequency with which you will communicate and the method by which you will communicate. This planning process is very important because it provides the project manager with a structure to follow and a checklist so that he can ensure that all appropriate stakeholders have been informed of relevant information at the appropriate time. There is much more, however, to communication and we are now going to look at some of the softer sides of communication.

QUESTIONS FOR REFLECTION

1.   Are you clear about which stakeholders in particular you need to engage?

2.   Are you confident that you understand their preferences with regard to communication technologies and frequency?

3.   Does your communication plant take account of differing stakeholder preferences?

4.   Have you allocated sufficient time to ensure that the messages that you need to communicate will be sufficiently informing and engaging?

Communication is a Human Behaviour

All human behaviour in all situations is affected by three factors: our perceptions, cognitions and emotions. Communication is a human behaviour and is consequently affected by these three things.

PERCEPTION

At the risk of sounding philosophical and 'airy fairy', I would just like to make the point that there is no such thing as objective 'reality'. We all have our own version of 'reality' based on our experiences, our personality, our level of knowledge and skill and so on. George Kelly (1963) suggested that we each look at the world and situations through our own particular goggles and that the world and various situations look different to each of us; in other words, we all perceive things differently. This can lead to new insights and creativity, which is great; however, our perceptions can lead us to distort events. These distortions can, on occasions, prevent us from perceiving something in a clear and rational way.

WHAT IS PERCEPTION?

Lewicki et al. (2007) define 'perception' as 'the process by which individuals connect to their environment.' The process of ascribing meaning to messages and events is strongly influenced by the perceiver's current state of mind, role and comprehension of any earlier communications/experiences. Other parties' perceptions, the environment and the perceiver's own disposition are also important influences on one's ability to interpret with accuracy what the other party is saying and meaning. Human beings have a tremendous capacity for processing information which is still unmatched by any computer, despite the leaps in technological advances. Because we have this capacity to input so much information, evolution has provided us with shortcuts to organise this information and these can sometimes cause us to make wide generalisations or distortions which can lead to mistakes. The distortions are stereotyping, the 'horns and halo' effect, selective perception and attribution.

STEREOTYPING

In order to reduce the burden that processing information plays on our cognitive systems, we human beings have evolved a system where we assume a whole range of attributes about a person and 'pigeon-hole' them accordingly. This attribution is usually based on very little information – for example, a person's age, gender, ethnicity, accent, mode of dress and so on. This 'pigeon-hole' process tends to group people together and assume that they are all similar. To take an example, we may meet someone at a party and because they are dressed in something slightly unusual for the event, we may stereotype them as being 'eccentric' and from this we may assume that they are probably quite untidy, won't get on well with most people, probably very intelligent and creative but perhaps a bit of a geek. If we were to test out any of these assumptions, it is highly likely that they would all be incorrect, but unfortunately we do not often take the time to test our assumptions. We assume that we know all about that person and this then affects the way in which we interact with them. To take the example that we have used of someone being stereotyped as 'eccentric' we may decide that they are too 'off the wall for us' and thus refrain from interacting with them. Alternatively, we may decide that individuality is refreshing and feel that we want to spend time getting to know them better.

This same 'stereotyping' process occurs within the business environment and also has an impact on the type of people that we choose to invest our time in. This could cause us to miss out on some potentially good relationships and it is important that project managers learn to question their stereotypical perceptions and test out their assumptions about stakeholders and so on. This testing process is very important because, as Lewicki et al. (2007) emphasise, once formed, stereotypes are highly resistant to change. When meeting stakeholders, project managers should try to avoid making any sweeping judgements about the stakeholder and concentrate on what they actually do know about the person based on what they have said about themselves. This then allows the project manager to engage in active listening (as discussed in Chapter 5) and form a more accurate understanding of the stakeholder.

THE 'HORNS AND HALO' EFFECT

This distortion has nothing to do with fancy dress as the slightly whimsical name seems to suggest. Instead, it refers to the fact that if we see people performing well on one task or in one situation, we generalise this to everything else and assume that they are good at everything; for example, if we see a team member playing golf well, we may assume that he is good at everything else. This is the 'halo' effect. Conversely, if we see someone doing one thing badly, we may generalise this to other situations and assume that he is not very good at a range of things. This is the 'horns' effect. As you can see, this distortion has much in common with 'stereotyping' but once again it is worth being aware of these tendencies and trying to ensure that you are not being swayed by one particularly good or bad example of a stakeholder or team member's behaviour. In Chapter 5, we talked about utilising a coaching approach to gain a deeper understanding of stakeholders and their requirements. Remember that it helps to have a belief in people's potential and be aware of falling into the 'halo and horns' effect. If you succumb to the 'horns' effect, you could find yourself mentally writing off someone who could be a great asset to your project. Conversely, if you succumb to the 'halo' effect, you could find yourself putting too much trust in someone or even giving someone a level of task and responsibility that they are not ready for. Either of the above could prove detrimental to your project.

SELECTIVE PERCEPTION

This perceptual distortion serves to reinforce our stereotypes and 'horns and halo' effect, in that, we tend to form an opinion about someone using the latter two and then carefully (but not consciously) select out any information in what the individual does or says that confirms our original suspicion. We tend to ignore anything that contradicts or challenges it. This tends to be a particularly unhelpful distortion as it takes us further and further away from a more realistic appraisal of the individual in question which can have a very detrimental impact on project relationships.

ATTRIBUTION THEORY

This perceptual distortion is about what we attribute other people's behaviour to; for example, if a team member fails to achieve a task, there are a number of possible reasons as to why this may have happened. It does not take Einstein to realise that if we attribute this apparent failure to the fact that the team member's PC was faulty we are going to feel rather different about that individual than if we believe that the failure was down to a lack of intelligence or skill on his part. Once again, the trick is to be aware that we are all capable of engaging in these distortions and try to guard against them.

QUESTIONS FOR REFLECTION

1.	Are you making judgements based on your perceptions or stereotypes?

2.	What checks could you put in place to ensure that you are being objective rather than judgemental?

3.	To what extent do you think that your attitude and behaviour towards someone could be disproportionately influenced by a previous event or opinion that you hold?

Non-Verbal Communication

So we have looked at some of the intrapersonal processes that might have an impact on the type of communication that we use to engage with stakeholders. Let's look now at some of the interpersonal processes, that is, those aspects of our communication that other people see. The anthropologist Ray L. Birdwhistell suggested that less than 35 per cent of the message in conversations is conveyed verbally whilst the remaining 65 per cent is communicated non-verbally. This suggestion was supported by additional research indicating that in face-to-face interactions:

•	7 per cent of the meaning is derived from the words spoken

- 38 per cent from tone of voice, loudness, and other aspects of how things are said

- 55 per cent from facial expressions

These figures suggest that we should pay more attention to the way in which we say something than what we actually say.

VOICE AND TONE

These are two factors that are important to be aware of if you wish to communicate successfully. When we do not agree with what someone else is saying often a note of disapproval or challenge creeps into our voice and this is very easily detected by the listener. How many times have you had a major argument with your teenage son or daughter because they think you do not approve of their friends? Chances are that, however positive your comments about the friend were, your niggling doubts would have been present in your tone. The volume at which we communicate something can also have a significant impact on how our messages are received by others; for example, when we are angry we tend to increase the volume of our voice, consequently, if you are communicating in a loud tone, your recipients may assume that you are angry even if you are not.

When communicating, it is useful to adopt a calm and measured tone of voice so as not to convey any feelings of our own impatience. This avoids any defensive reactions and facilitates a more rational and even discussion. One way in which we can help train our voices to calmness is by being curious. When we are intrigued or curious about something, our voices become slower and more melodic. Consequently, one technique you could use when you meet a stakeholder is to ask yourself questions beforehand about him; for example, what does he do in his spare time, where does he go for his holidays, what kind of person is he really? This mental curiosity should result in your voice being calm even when you do speak. This is a particularly useful technique when you have to convey a difficult message or one that you know is likely to meet with serious opposition. It also has the added bonus of slightly lowering your own levels of tension, in that it momentarily distracts you and avoids you focusing on potentially negative outcomes to the discussion.

FACIAL EXPRESSIONS

We often pick up clues about how other people are feeling from the facial expressions that they adopt; for example, if someone is grimacing all the way through your 'pitch', you might well assume that they are going to object to your proposal. The best advice with regard to facial expressions is – smile frequently. Smiling will make you feel positive and it will also facilitate a positive environment. In Chapter 2, we talked about emotional intelligence and how our moods transfer to people around us. This is true of smiling, in that smiling tends to elicit a smiling response from others.

PROXEMICS

This is a complicated-sounding word but it simply refers to the space in which communication takes place – for example, whether it takes place in the project manager's office or the office of one of the stakeholders. Equally, proxemics is about personal distance, that is, the amount of physical distance that we like to keep between others and ourselves when we are communicating. Proxemics are a useful thing to bear in mind in your communication strategy, particularly where you have important or controversial messages to convey. You may wish to choose a venue where your audience will feel comfortable and relaxed in order to minimise any potential tension. This venue could be the stakeholder's desk or it could be a more neutral venue such as the staff coffee room. Do be aware of how close you are standing to the people you are conveying a message to. This is particularly important for those project managers with either impressive height or breadth as if you stand too close to others it can be perceived as somewhat threatening. Furhnam (2000) suggests that a distance of between 4 and 12 feet is about right for a social or business encounter. In addition, you may also want to remember that people feel more collaborative when you talk to them from a similar height so if you are really tall, you may choose to sit down in order to communicate your message.

BODY LANGUAGE

I think that most people now are aware of the basic *dos* and *don'ts* around body language so I do not intend to dwell much on this. Basically, there are certain body postures that are more conducive to a positive and open discussion – for example, not having your arms folded, which is often perceived as a closed and defensive position. Uncrossed legs also suggest an open and non-defensive position.

PERSONAL APPEARANCE AND MANNERISMS

Part of our survival heritage from our ancestors is the tendency to make quick decisions about new situations and very quickly pigeon-hole them. This helps us identify the extent to which something is a threat and save cognitive time by allocating it to the nearest comparable mental compartment. This means that we tend to make snap decisions about people we meet and use our pre-existing 'pigeon-holes' to determine where they best fit. In other words, we make a large number of assumptions about people based on very little real information. This means that if you want to make a good impression on people and win them over, there are certain factors that you need to take into account. First of all the way you dress, that is, how you look to people. Do you look how others expect a project manager to look? This may seem superficial but how we appear to others does have an impact on the amount of credibility we create in their eyes. Secondly, how do you come across to people? Do you have a warm, assertive manner or are you always slightly apologetic? Do you have any particular mannerism? For example, do you always run your fingers through your hair when you appear to be losing an argument?

The way in which we dress and the types of gestures that we make are part and parcel of who we are. They make us individual and I would not suggest that anyone lose any aspect of their individuality. Unfortunately, however, people do judge us by these superficial things and it is another aspect of your communication repertoire that you may wish to give some consideration to.

Using Non-Verbal Communication to Create a Positive Atmosphere for Communication

CREATING RAPPORT THROUGH MIRRORING

Throughout the section on non-verbal communication we have made reference to creating a positive mood for a face-to-face communication exercise. We are now going to look at how to use non-verbal techniques to improve the impact of your spoken message.

One technique that is widely used in coaching to facilitate rapport is a technique known as 'mirroring'. If you have ever observed two old friends chatting, you will probably have noticed a number of things. Firstly, they will probably have been looked very relaxed in each other's company and they probably appeared to be in a good mood. You may well have noticed that their body language was either very similar or identical. When we trust and like someone and feel comfortable with them, we tend to mirror their body language; for example, if they lean forward, we lean forward. If they put their head on one side, we put our head on one side and so on.

This is something that we do subconsciously and quite naturally and it is perceived subconsciously by the other person as a feeling of positive regard and liking. This 'mirroring' is not only limited to gesture either, people tend to match each other's tone of voice and speed of conversation. Although mirroring usually takes place at a subconscious level, it can actually be used consciously as a way of creating a more positive rapport between two people. The trick when doing this consciously is to keep it simple and to a minimum or the other person will see that you are deliberately copying them and may think that you are taking the proverbial or that you are pretty weird. A useful way forward in trying to create a positive rapport would be to observe the body language of the stakeholder/team member and then imitate one or two gestures; for example, if the other person cups their chin on their hand, imitate them. If the other person sits slightly angled to the side, sit at the same angle. This will help create a feeling of collaboration.

OTHER WAYS OF CREATING A POSITIVE ENVIRONMENT

There are several other things that you can do to start any discussion or negotiation off on a positive footing. Firstly, smiling and nodding and standing/sitting close to the other party to the discussion helps create a feeling of empathy (bearing in mind the points we made about proximity earlier in this chapter). Secondly, sitting or standing in an open position, that is, no legs or arms crossed, also helps create a feeling of openness and trust. Being patient and allowing the other party sufficient time to speak without interrupting will also create a positive vibe along with actively listening (remember we discussed active listening in Chapter 5) to what is being said and showing this attention through good eye contact and making listening noises, for example, 'mm', ' I see' (Parsloe and Wray 2003).

A NOTE OF CAUTION

Don't become so distracted by the non-verbal aspects of communication that you miss out on the actual content of the message. Do, however, try to become more observant with regard to the non-verbal aspects of communication and use them not only to pick up on indications of how the other person is responding to your message but also to help you create a rapport to facilitate good communication between you and your stakeholders/team.

Using Transactional Analysis (TA) to Improve Your Communication Techniques

USING TRANSACTIONAL ANALYSIS TO UNDERSTAND HOW TEAM MEMBERS RELATE TO EACH OTHER

We talked about Transactional Analysis (TA) in Chapter 3 when we looked at using it to help build your project team. We talked about communicating from one of three states: the child (id), the adult (ego) or the parent (superego). Remember that the 'adult' state is considered to be the most effective medium for interpersonal interaction.

By observing a team member during a discussion or interaction with someone, it is possible to get an indication of which ego state the individual is operating from because parent states usually include judging words and child words are usually more spontaneous and direct. The table overleaf provides an indication of the type of words, voice and attitude that typically characterise each ego state.

Questions for Reflection

1. Are you aware of your non-verbal communication and the impact that it has on others?

2. Are you aware of the non-verbal communication that other people use whom you regularly interact with?

3. Are you using non-verbal communication to your advantage?

4. Are there particular types of situations where you feel that you could improve your communication?

5. What steps could you take to ensure that your communication is effective?

Table 6.1 Behavioural clues as to which TA state the individual is operating from (Woollams and Brown 1979)

Controlling parent	Nurturing parent	Adult	Free child	Adapted child
Uses punitive words, e.g. 'Bad', 'Should', 'Ridiculous'	Uses words such as 'Good', 'Nice'	Uses words such as 'How', 'What', 'Why'	Uses words such as 'Fun', 'Want'	Uses words such as 'Can't', 'Wish'
Critical	Comforting	Precise	Loud	Whining
Angry	Accepting	Thoughtful	Uninhibited	Pouting
Judgemental	Understanding	Interested	Fun-loving	Demanding

7

Managing Risk in Projects

The issue of risk is a crucial one in project management and many definitions of project management refer to the management of risks. There are different categories of risk associated with projects – for example, risk of failure, risk of going over budget, risk of not completing on time, risk of not satisfying the project board and/or stakeholders. There are also the decisions throughout the life of the project that incur risks of varying proportions and consequences. If you Google the topic 'risk management' or visit any library with a business or academic section, you will quickly realise that 'risk management' has become a discipline in its own right. There are professional bodies who oversee the discipline of 'risk management' such as the UK-based 'Institute of Risk Management (IRM)' and the 'Association of Insurance and Risk Managers AIRMIC' to name but two. 'Risk management' has its own body of knowledge and there are also various professional qualifications that one can attain. In addition, there are various software tools that are available to help project manager's model and eliminate/manage risk.

Given that there is already a huge body of academic (and not so academic) texts on the subject of risk management in projects we are not going to spend much time on this; instead, we are going to look at risk from a more human angle and explore the psychology of risk. From the literature on project management and risk management there appears to be a belief that mathematical formulas and logical linear thinking will be sufficient to effectively manage risk. There appears to be little credence given to the unique contribution that individuals bring to the management of risk. In fact, the general assumption appears to be that as long as project team members are aware of the risk management plan then the appropriate decision will be made or appropriate action taken which reduces or eliminates the risk. The relatively high failure rate of projects suggests that risk management is not as straightforward as this and perhaps more attention needs to be paid to the human element of risk.

The Human Element of Risk Management

BARINGS BANK

One of the most stark modern-day examples of the dangers of not managing risk must be the example of 'Barings Bank'. Barings Bank recruited a new employee by the name of Nick Leeson and owing to his impressive performance he was quickly appointed to the trade floor where he appeared to be making large amounts of money for the bank. The bank did not believe that it was taking any risk as Nick assured them that he was speculating on behalf of a client. Unfortunately, Nick was very good at hiding his losses and the bank only found out that there was a problem when Nick's losses exceeded the bank's overall reserves and capital. This oversight brought about the collapse of the oldest merchant bank in London and sent shockwaves throughout the entire financial community.

THE THREE ELEMENTS OF HUMAN BEHAVIOUR

There are essentially three elements of human behaviour that need to be considered in association with any risk management process: individual factors, group factors and organisational factors. Individual factors include the individual's psychological disposition toward risk, their understanding of alternative courses of action and consequences and their psychological approach to decision-making. 'Group factors' include the team environment and 'organisational factors' refer to the wider cultural expectations and attitude towards failure.

Individual Factors

Since the much publicised works of Sigmund Freud, psychologists have studied the human psyche and tried to measure the various traits that comprise the human personality. Over time, these measurements have become more accurate and a body of knowledge has built up based on research evidence. The research has demonstrated that human personality – that is, our disposition towards ourselves, others and the world at large – can be measured along a continuum on a number of dimensions. Some of these dimensions are highly relevant to the study and management of project risk management.

An experimental study by Moràn et al. (2003) found that those who took the most risks knew least about the risks that they were taking. This is a little worrying, particularly when you consider the millions of pounds at stake in some projects, not to mention reputation, and so on.

A study by Jose and Crumly (1993, reported in Weigel 2000) investigated the influence that personality has on the degree of financial risk that an individual is willing to take. This research was carried out with American farmers. Jose and Crumly used the 'Myers Briggs Type Indicator' (MBTI) with farmers to assess their personality type. The 'MBTI' is an instrument for assessing personality based on the work of Karl Jung and we discussed it in Chapter 3 when we looked at tools and techniques for teambuilding. Based on the completion of a questionnaire they found that 65 per cent of the farmers were sensing/thinking types (SJs) and only 6 per cent were intuitive/thinking types (NTs). Jose and Crumly found that the 'SJs' reached the same conclusions about which techniques or practices to adopt as the 'NTs' but they chose less risky approaches than the NTs. This suggests that personality does play a part in the types of risks that we are willing to take and the extent to which we will take risks, as individuals.

Nicholson et al. (2002) carried out research into risk and the role that personality factors play in the extent to which we are prepared to take risks. They found that risk behaviour is patterned; that is, some people are likely to be consistent risk takers, some are consistently risk-averse and some are willing to take risks in some areas of their life but not all.

They also found that people who took higher levels of risk tended to be more extrovert than average and scored higher on 'openness' (being open to new ideas and experiences). High risk takers also scored lower on neuroticism (being prone to experience the more negative emotions such as anxiety and anger) and agreeableness (being cooperative and compassionate with others) indicating that they have less emotional intelligence and are less concerned about the impact on others or about what other people think. They also scored lower on conscientiousness (being self-disciplined and dutiful) and therefore cared less about the methods by which they achieved something. Nicholson et al. (2002) suggest that people who are conscientious will strive to achieve in a disciplined way, whereas people who score low on 'conscientiousness' are more likely to have a 'get rich quick' mentality which leads them to take risks.

It can be seen then that there are individual personality factors that play a role in the extent to which people are likely to be risk takers or risk avoidant. Obviously other elements also have an influence, for example the individual's perception of the risk. In an ideal world, people would have evidence regarding the probability of the risk occurring and its likely impact. In the real world, however, there is often little information about the probability of a risk occurring or its potential impact. Consequently, people have to resort to subjective judgements in order to manage the risk. Obviously, the more familiar someone is with the probable risk, the more likely they are to provide a realistic assessment. Research has shown that people are poorer at estimating risk levels for highly improbable risks, probably because they have no experience on which to base their subjective estimates. In reality, it is likely that most risk management plans are based more on guesstimate than estimate, which means that the risk management plan alone cannot be relied upon to manage risk. Project managers would benefit from knowing something about the individual project team member's approach to risk.

DECISION-MAKING

There is an additional risk factor associated with the individual characteristics of project team members and that is around their decision-making style. Individual personality factors influence the speed with which individuals make decisions and consequently the time that they will take to both gather and evaluate information. This is important because if there is a crucial decision to make, you are more likely to make the right one if you have sufficient information about alternatives and consequences, and if you are able to accurately evaluate this information in the time available.

Isobel Briggs Myers was one of the founders of the 'Myers Briggs Type Indicator' (MBTI), which we looked at in Chapter 3. We saw that the main dimensions utilised were *thinking* vs *Feeling, extroversion* vs *introversion, judgement* vs *perception*; and *sensing* vs *intuition*. Isobel Briggs Myers suggested that an individual's scores on these dimensions would indicate their decision-making style. To take an example, if an individual scored near the thinking, extroversion, sensing, and judgement ends of the dimensions he or she would tend to have a logical, analytical approach to decision-making. If, however, an individual scored at the 'feeling' and 'intuitive' end of the dimensions, he or she is likely to be swayed more by the opinions of others than by hard facts. Other personality measures also have something to offer on individual differences in the decision-making process; for example, the 'occupational personality questionnaire (OPQ)' indicates whether an individual is likely to take their time in making a decision and consider all facts, or whether they will make a decision very quickly. Various studies have also indicated that there are cultural differences in decision-making which project managers will have to take into account if they are managing a global project or if there are project team members of different nationalities.

Our personality differences and experiences in life also result in certain cognitive biases that we adopt when making decisions; for example, we can be selective in our search for evidence and subconsciously only choose evidence that supports our preferred conclusion. We may also finish our search for evidence prematurely if we find evidence that looks as though it might support a conclusion without exploring further to see if there is a better match. We can also be resistant to change (something that we will be exploring in Chapter 9) which means that we may not look outside the box and consequently miss information which could help us better manage a risk.

Group Factors That Influence the Management of Project Risk

The behaviour of groups such as project teams can have an influence on the effectiveness with which project risk is managed. There are some group behaviours that facilitate good risk management, and equally others that do the opposite. Let's start by looking at the unhelpful group behaviours.

GROUPTHINK

One of the best examples of an unhelpful group behaviour is 'groupthink' which we discussed in Chapter 3. This is where the group agrees on a decision without a full appraisal of the facts or consequences. It is easy to see how a project team operating in this mode is unlikely to successfully manage risk.

RISKY SHIFT

Risky shift is a phenomenon first discovered by Stoner (1961) when he was looking at risk taking in groups. He found that groups made decisions that were much higher risk than decisions made individually by the members of the group. There have been many theories over the years as to why this might be the case; however, the two leading schools of thought suggest that 'Risky shift' is due to either 'persuasive argument theory' or 'social comparison theory'. 'Persuasive argument theory' proposes that individuals are swayed by the arguments of others and may consequently be persuaded to take a riskier decision that they would not have taken on their own. Personality factors would impact on this as some people are more inclined to be swayed by the feelings and opinions of others. 'Social comparison theory' describes the human tendency to want to appear socially desirable to others. In other words, people in groups will often go with the favoured majority rather than stick to their own views. This may result in a less than optimum decision being made which increases risk.

TEAM CULTURE

In Chapter 3, we looked at building teams and developing effective team cultures. We saw then that some aspects of team culture can be unhelpful to team cooperation and therefore unhelpful to the management of projects and risk. One example is where team members try to maintain a position of always being 'the expert'. This is unhelpful because 'the expert' will fail to discuss issues with the team as s/he will not wish to lose 'the expert' status. Equally, other team members may be afraid to challenge 'the expert' for fear of looking foolish. Teams with this type of approach are unlikely to manage risk well and actually pose a risk in their own right. Project managers will need to monitor the levels of authority and decision-making that they delegate to individuals within the project team to ensure that everyone's views are valued and that an 'expert culture' is not created.

Impersonal teams and/or teams where individuals defend their own interests are also unlikely to manage risk particularly well. Project managers will need to encourage a team culture where project team members value group participation and support each other, such as by using the 'team roles' framework developed by Belbin that we saw in Chapter 3. A project manager should try and ensure that he has a 'chairman' who will try to ensure that everyone is able to make a contribution to the decision, a 'shaper' who is always ready to challenge, a 'resource investigator' who will look outside the box and a 'monitor/evaluator' who will be able to exercise judgement in a clear and unemotional way.

COMMUNICATION STYLE

The communication style of the project team can also have an impact on risk. Ideally, a project team should discuss and evaluate information in order to reach an appropriate and well-balanced decision that successfully manages project risk. Unfortunately, most project teams are not perfect communicators and this provides an extra layer of risk to be managed. Communication styles that reduce risk are those where the team is:

- open and honest with each other

- comfortable in challenging each other's assumptions and decisions

- able to receive challenge in an open minded way without becoming defensive

Organisational Factors That Impact on Risk Management

There are numerous aspects of organisational life that potentially influence the way in which risk is managed in an organisation. These organisational factors can be subsumed under the heading of 'organisational culture'. Organisational culture has been defined in many ways but perhaps one of the most well-known definitions is that offered by Schein (1993):

> *A pattern of shared basic assumptions that the group learned as it solved its problems of external adaptation and internal integration, that has worked well enough to be considered valid and therefore, to be taught to new members as the correct way to perceive, think, and feel in relation to those problems.*

Culture is not always a uniform thing within organisations, in that there may be a dominant culture which pervades all aspects of organisational life but individual departments and even teams can have their own particular culture (known as a 'subculture') although the significant aspects are likely to be congruent with the dominant culture – for example, attitudes to reward and failure. As we discussed in Chapter 3, project teams often have slightly different cultures from the rest of the organisation as project teams can be very specific and focused.

The aspects of culture that have the most impact on how risk is managed within an organisation tend to be the following:

1.   Type of leadership.

2.   Attitude towards blame.

3.   Attitude towards reward.

4.   Attitude towards challenge.

5.   Attitude towards support.

6.   Attitude towards asking for help/mentoring.

7.   Attitude towards power.

TYPE OF LEADERSHIP

We looked at leadership in Chapter 2, so I do not intend to say to too much about this topic. The main point to make is that the leadership of an organisation is a significant factor in determining the organisational culture of the organisation. Obviously, some types of leadership are more conducive to the effective management of project risk than others. This is because the type of leadership utilised within an organisation determines factors two to six, listed above.

ATTITUDE TOWARDS BLAME

Organisations differ in the extent to which they have a blame culture and also in the types of behaviours and attitudes that they reward either financially or non-financially. Both of these are important factors in the management of project risk. The online encyclopedia 'Encarta' defines a blame culture as:

> *A set of attitudes, for example, within a business organisation, characterised by an unwillingness to take risks or accept responsibility for mistakes because of a fear of criticism or prosecution.*

Blame cultures are characterised by finger-pointing and when anything does not work as well as it should have done, the first question asked is 'Who is to blame? Whose fault is this?' This is an extremely unhelpful approach for any organisation in any industry because it creates a culture of fear. Individuals within organisations of this nature tend to keep their heads down and do not offer any new ideas or suggestions for fear of getting 'shot down'. Individuals tend always to take the 'safe' route as highly likely to be the way that the organisation reacted to the situation the last time that it occurred – as long as the approach was successful, of course. Unfortunately, what appears to be the 'safe' route may not always be the best route in the long term and could potentially expose the organisation or project to a higher level of risk in the long term. In addition, this type of organisational culture stifles creativity.

Another problem with 'blame cultures' is that individuals do not feel able to admit that something is not working and will hide mistakes rather than expose themselves to punishment. This prevents organisational learning and the effective management of risk.

The issue of 'reward' is linked in with 'blame cultures' in that individuals in organisations that have this type of culture will only be rewarded for successes. This sounds sensible at face value until you start thinking about what this actually means. Success within a 'blame culture' is likely to be limited and lack innovation.

ATTITUDE TOWARDS REWARD

I would like to offer a slightly cautionary view on this particular aspect of culture, in that organisations tend to be on a continuum in the extent to which they reward risk taking and innovation. At the one end, you may have the financial services sector which is now probably somewhat adverse to risk, given the Barings Bank incident and the current economic climate, and at the other end of the scale you may have companies such as Dyson which actively encourage and reward risk taking despite it not always being a raging success. I think that there are dangers at both ends of the spectrum. If you have a company that does not reward risk taking then you may put a project at risk by taking a low-risk route that could potentially have a negative impact on the project. At the other end of the spectrum, if you have company that encourages risk taking, then you may encourage serial risk takers who take a risk for the sake of it as opposed to it being a calculated decision.

ATTITUDE TOWARDS CHALLENGE

All organisations differ in the extent to which challenging others is acceptable; for example, is it appropriate for one colleague to gently probe the decision-making processes of another colleague? Is it acceptable for a subordinate to question a decision made by their supervisor or manager? In some organisations it is unacceptable for a subordinate to challenge a manager, perhaps because of the organisational culture or the attitude of individual managers. Unfortunately, this is very unhelpful for the management of risk, as risk is reduced when team members are able to challenge each other's decision-making in an open and non-threatening manner. 'Challenge', when utilised well, facilitates the exploration and evaluation of information and helps people to check that they are interpreting it in the right way and making the correct assumptions.

ATTITUDE TOWARDS SUPPORT

Another cultural aspect in which organisations differ is the extent to which support is encouraged within the organisation; for example, are team members expected to support each other, or are people left to sink? People are less likely to take an appropriate risk if they do not feel that anyone else in the team will support them.

ATTITUDE TOWARDS ASKING FOR HELP AND MENTORING

Those organisations where it is culturally acceptable to ask for help without it being seen as a weakness are more likely to facilitate an environment where team/project team members take appropriate risks. The facility of being able to check something with someone else without being made to feel like an idiot is extremely useful, particularly in the management of risk. Similarly, those organisations that have mentors are more likely to encourage people to step outside their comfort zone and take an appropriate risk.

ATTITUDE TOWARDS POWER

Organisations can differ considerably in the extent and pattern in which power is distributed. Earlier in this chapter we talked about the problems that can potentially occur when you have an 'expert' culture with one person appearing to have more power than others. Similarly, there are still organisations where information is seen as power and individuals hoard information and knowledge because they think it gives them an edge in some way. Obviously this is unhelpful in the context of risk management as it means some project team members could be taking decisions without being in possession of the relevant facts.

So How Can a Project Manager More Effectively Manage Risk?

Research has shown that people are more likely to take risks where they feel supported, there is a no-blame culture and they are trusted/empowered to take those risks. Consequently, project managers should try to facilitate a risk management culture where all those things are in place. In addition, it is necessary that the project manager understand something about the attitude to risk held by the individual project team members, and the best way to do this is by taking the time to get to know team members and discover how they approach risk and decision-making. There are personality measures and team role measures that can help you with this if you only have limited time to spend with team members or if they are too far spread geographically.

Project managers should also implement processes to ensure that effective communication takes place within/between teams and that information is shared where appropriate. In addition, project managers should implement a proper evaluation process to ensure that information and decisions within the project team are suitably challenged and explored. There may be a need to support team members with the process of challenging each other and some team members may take time to build up their confidence to do this, particularly if they have a more introverted personality style. The project manager will need to monitor decision-making in the short term to ensure that the above processes are happening and that they are working effectively.

8

Managing Conflict in Projects

Working life can be fraught with conflict, some of which is easy to resolve and some of which takes a lot more time and effort. Unfortunately, project management has a huge propensity for conflict simply because there are numerous interdependent relationships and projects often cross organisational and managerial boundaries. In addition the often tight time constraints of project activities can bring project teams into conflict with stakeholders who also have to deliver day-to-day business as well (often this is true of the project team itself who may have to deliver their role in the project over and above their day-to-day jobs). Because of this, it is very useful for project managers to be able to anticipate likely conflict, but more importantly to be able to deal with conflict when it does occur in a way that promotes harmony and the achievement of project targets.

So what do we mean by conflict? Essentially conflict is a difference of opinion between individuals or groups of people which may be about a divergence of interests or could simply be opposition to the other's plans or aspirations. The generally held view is that conflict is a bad thing and something to be avoided at all costs. This can be true on occasions; however, conflict can actually be a positive thing for a number or reasons. Conflict can highlight weaknesses in plans and result in more effective solutions being produced. It also facilitates discussion and brings feelings/emotions to the forefront. This is sometimes cathartic and allows someone to get something off their chest. The advantage of this for a project manager is that at least you know what you are dealing with and it is much easier to deal with opposition once it is out in the open. The trick then is to understand what the conflict is about and deal with it positively.

The Structure of Conflict

According to Bradford University (2000), all conflicts have certain basic elements in common. They all generally involve attitudes, behaviours and structures and these three elements tend to be interlinked. *Attitudes* include the parties' perceptions and misperceptions of each other and of themselves. These can be positive or negative. Attitudes are often influenced by emotions such as fear, anger, bitterness and hatred. *Behaviours* can include cooperation or coercion, gestures signifying conciliation or hostility. *Structures* refer to the political mechanisms and processes within organisations. Conflict is a dynamic process in which structure, attitudes and behaviours are constantly changing and influencing one another.

THE TYPES OF CONFLICT

There are essentially four different types of conflict which Lewicki et al. (2007) define as intrapersonal, interpersonal, intergroup, and intragroup.

Intrapersonal conflict

This term describes the internal conflict that we experience from time to time, for example where we are asked to carry out a piece of work that clashes with our own personal value system. This is probably the area of conflict that will be of least concern to a project manager.

Interpersonal conflict

This is about conflict between individuals which is a fairly common occurrence within organisations and within project management. An example of this would be where the operations manager constantly makes negative comments about your project plan and refuses to cooperate.

Intragroup conflict

This is about conflict within a team or a group; for example, one member of the project team may be antagonistic towards one or all of the remaining team members.

Intergroup conflict

This is where two groups are at odds with each other. An example of this would be where the finance department refuse to cooperate with your project during March/April as they say they have to get the end-of-year accounts finished. This would put your project team in conflict with the finance department if you had project elements that you needed the finance department to complete during that time period.

Conflict can occur for a number of reasons. It could arise as a result of a fundamental difference of opinion or simply a misunderstanding or misperception of a situation or event. Conflict can also occur when people are working towards the same ends but perhaps want slightly different things out of the end product or service. Conflict can become very emotional and very ugly and I am sure that we have all witnessed at least some of the downsides mentioned below (Lewicki et al. 2006).

THE DOWNSIDE OF CONFLICT

Going into competition – people lose sight of the interdependencies necessary for the project and start to act as though they are totally independent. They can, on occasions, even start to compete with each other.

Distorted thinking errors – thinking loses some of its logic and some of the thinking errors that we discussed in Chapter 7 start to creep in – for example, stereotyping, selective perception (people only pay attention to things that support their argument), projection (they project their own motives and feelings onto others and misinterpret their rationale for doing and saying things). Generally speaking, there is a certain amount of misperception going on.

Emotional hijack – as conflict heightens, situations become more emotional and negative emotions start to make a presence – for example, irritation, anger, hostility, and so on.

Withdrawal – the quality of communication tends to decline during conflict situations to the point where parties may just avoid communicating with each other. Alternatively the only communication that takes place tends to be negative.

Blurring the edges – the emotional context of conflict can lead people to lose sight of what the key issues really are and this can sometimes lead to the introduction of various red herrings.

Polar opposition – the more serious occurrences of conflict can lead to parties to the conflict magnifying their differences and splitting into two totally opposed camps 'where never the twain shall meet'.

Entrenchment – this is where the conflict has become prolonged and people become entrenched in their own positions. It goes without saying that there is more chance of dealing positively and effectively with conflict if it is tackled in the early stages. As people become more entrenched, relationships start to break down and it is a much more difficult job to bring about a degree of harmony. This situation could be absolutely catastrophic to a project, if interdependent tasks are not delivered on time.

Some of the strategies that we looked at in 'managing negotiation' will be very helpful to project managers dealing with conflict, for example the 'principled negotiation' that we discussed in Chapter 5. In addition, three are a number of other techniques that you can use to help you create mutual goals and build good relationships, for example, Transactional Analysis (see Chapter 3 and 'Coaching' as we discussed in Chapter 5). We will proceed later on in the chapter to look at how these techniques can be used to help manage conflict.

Addressing Conflict

CONFLICT SETTLEMENT

For many years, the attention of conflict researchers and theorists was directed to the laudable objective of conflict settlement. This is where the focus is on reaching an agreement between parties. Usually this involved one or both parties compromising in some way in order to reach a harmonious agreement. This can be an effective way of removing conflict but not always. In a project management context, any compromises reached could affect the successful delivery of the project or the ability of the project team to deliver the project on time and within budgets. The following anecdote from Fisher and Ury (1981) about two sisters and an orange illustrates why compromise may not always be the most effective option.

The two sisters and the orange

Each would like the entire orange. The solution is to split it 50–50 which, although is fair, is not necessarily wise. One sister proceeds to peel the orange, discard the peel and eat her half of the fruit; the other peels the orange, discards the fruit, and uses her part of the peel to bake a cake.

CONFLICT RESOLUTION

Over the years there has been a gradual shift towards conflict resolution as opposed to conflict settlement. In conflict resolution the focus is not solely about reaching an agreement. Conflict resolution is a more involved approach which facilitates mutual sharing between the parties in conflict. It focuses on addressing the roots of conflict and changing attitudes so that behaviour changes and relationships become less hostile and more favourable. Bradford University (2000) suggest that the process of conflict resolution includes becoming aware of a conflict, diagnosing its nature and applying appropriate methods in order to:

- diffuse the negative emotional energy involved;

- enable the disputing parties to understand and resolve their differences, so as to achieve solutions that are not imposed, which have been agreed by all the key parties, and which address the root causes of the conflict.

RECOGNISING CONFLICT

Of course it is necessary to recognise where conflict exists and you cannot deal with it if you do not know that it exists. Serious conflict is usually very visible and difficult to miss; however, by this point, key relationships may already have been soured or spoiled. Like a lot of things, conflict is often easier to resolve if it is caught in the early stages. There are usually warning signs that 'everything in the garden is not rosy' and it is important that project managers are vigilant and look for any signs that there is conflict. Some of the signs of conflict can be quite subtle:

- delays in responding to communications concerning the project

- persistent negativity

- 'us and them' mentality

- unwillingness to share information or ideas

- lack of interest in the project

- questioning everything

- pretending not to understand things that appear to be self-explanatory

When the elements listed above occur, it can be for very good reasons but any one of them or in fact any combination of them can also indicate negativity or the early warning signs of conflict.

USING CONFLICT TO FACILITATE TEAM GROWTH AND LEARNING

As we have seen in this chapter, there are a number of ways in which a project manager can address conflict and different strategies will be necessary according to which particular approach is taken. One option open to a project manager is to ignore any conflict which arises. There are occasions when this strategy can be successful; however, I would not personally recommend it as it can very easily undermine a project and turn into open hostility, as can be seen from the list of 'conflict downsides' listed earlier.

A second approach is to go down a conflict settlement path and compromise in order to reach a state or harmony. This approach can provide a fast and successful solution to conflict, but only in situations where compromise is possible without jeopardising the success of the project. The third route of conflict resolution offers the project manager an opportunity not only to resolve any emerging conflict but also to use the conflict as an opportunity to strengthen and develop the project team and its relationships with stakeholders. The tools and techniques used to bring about project resolution are the same regardless of whether the conflict is interpersonal, intergroup or intragroup in nature.

The Tools and Techniques of Conflict Resolution

ENLIGHTENED SELF-INTEREST

Breslin and Rubin (1989) suggests that one tool for bringing about conflict resolution is 'enlightened self interest'. This approach uses a combination of individualism and cooperation to allow you to move towards your objectives whilst making it possible for the other party to achieve theirs. At face value, this approach looks a little like the 'win/win' approach that we discussed in Chapter 5. I think that good conflict resolution should have 'win/win' at its core but it is important to remember that the key in resolving any conflict is to understand each party's underlying interests, needs and values instead of focusing on each party's positions. There are a number of techniques that we discussed in earlier chapters that you can use to help you resolve conflict and we will go on to explore how some of these techniques lend themselves well to conflict resolution.

USING A COACHING APPROACH TO RESOLVE CONFLICT

I would recommend overall that project managers use a coaching model to help them resolve conflict, for example the GROW model that we looked at in Chapter 4. Whichever coaching model is used the project manager should ensure that he engages in certain key processes: creating the right atmosphere, facilitating an open and honest exploration of the problem, exploring possible solutions which meet the needs of all parties, identifying mechanisms to support changes in behaviour/attitude, agreeing review processes/procedures to monitor progress.

CREATING A POSITIVE AND SUPPORTIVE ENVIRONMENT

It is important to bring the parties in conflict together in an environment that is conducive to resolving the conflict. It is usually better not to use an existing project meeting for this activity as you may need to create a little bit of distance from the project in order to encourage people to participate in your conflict resolution process. The timing of the meeting may need some consideration and you will need to think carefully about how you 'market' it to involved parties in order to ensure firstly that they attend and secondly that they will be open to discussion. In the following example where we look at using the 'GROW' model to resolve conflict, we will use the word 'party' to describe participants in the process. In the real world, those 'parties' could be team members, stakeholders or a mixture of team members and stakeholders, depending on the nature of the conflict.

USING THE 'GROW' MODEL TO RESOLVE CONFLICT

1.   *G* oal setting for the session as well as short-term and long-term

2.   *R* eality checking to explore the current situation

3.   *O* ptions and alternative strategies or courses of action

4.   *W* hat is to be done WHEN, by WHOM, and the WILL to do it

Remember that conflict is essentially about attitudes and behaviours which means that you need to encourage people to share their attitudes so that you can all understand why everyone is behaving in the way that they are and subsequently bring about change. A coaching approach such as the 'GROW' model provides project managers with a framework to explore the root causes of conflict by exploring how all parties think and feel about 'the problem' and facilitate individual and team development at the same time.

In Chapter 5 we also discussed Fisher and Ury (1991) and their model of 'principled negotiation'. Two of the four points identified in this model are a useful framework to have in the back of your mind when utilising the GROW model or any other method of conflict resolution:

- *Separate the person from the problem* – separate the problem from the person and jointly focus on the problem and how to resolve it.

- *Focus on interests not positions* – stakeholders are more likely to want to understand where you are coming from if you have demonstrated a genuine interest in their requirements.

The Stages of the Grow Model

GOAL-SETTING FOR THE SESSION AS WELL AS SHORT TERM AND LONG TERM

Use your first meeting as an opportunity to agree what it is that you all want to achieve, for example being able to work together more effectively (this is the 'G' part of the GROW model where you agree goals which can be short, long or medium term. It is worth establishing some common ground rules at this time):

- everyone is expected to express their views (this avoids people maintaining a position of silent resentfulness)

- no one speaks until the person expressing their views has finished

- everyone is treated with respect

- no name-calling

- any confidentialities will be respected

REALITY CHECKING TO EXPLORE THE CURRENT SITUATION

The next step is the 'reality check' which is where you encourage people to talk about what they see as 'the problem'. It is important at this stage to practice some of the key behaviours that we talked about in Chapter 5 as being necessary in interactions with stakeholders:

- relationship-building

- honesty and openness

- building shared ownership

- building understanding

The important thing at this stage is to find out what the conflict is really about, and in order to do this you need to encourage all parties to talk freely and openly about what they see as 'the problem'. Encourage people to share their feelings, that is, how does it make them feel when Joe Blogs does 'so and so'? As the facilitator of this meeting, the project manager will need to ensure that he engages in active listening and encourages others to do the same. There is no point in going through this process if you only intend to pay it lip-service as it will fail and potentially result in the conflict becoming more entrenched. You have to be prepared to take the time to really understand the needs of all parties and, although some project managers are tempted to try and rush through this process, you will gain more value and a deeper understanding by allowing sufficient time to fully explore issues. You will have to encourage some parties to open up and share their views as some people will naturally be more forthcoming than others. It is also a useful part of the process to encourage people to reflect by asking questions such as:

- So how do you feel about that now?

- Have Joe Blogs's comments made you feel any differently about him?

- Do you feel any differently about the problem now?

- What do you feel that you have gained from this discussion/ meeting?

Throughout the meeting, try to read the non-verbal signs of communication as well as taking note of what is actually said. This will give you a more accurate picture of the emotional environment. You will also need to use emotional intelligence to manage your own emotions and maintain a calm and neutral position, which will allow you to relate better to others. If you allow yourself to get caught up in the emotions of others, you will lose your objectivity and will lose the trust of some parties to the meeting. Thinking back to Chapter 3, when we looked at Transactional Analysis, try to maintain a position of 'I'm OK, You're OK' as this will help oil the wheels of communication and ensure a respectful and helpful dialogue. By avoiding disrespectful words and actions, you can resolve the problem faster

Working with emotions and feelings once they have been expressed

Some project managers are wary about asking people about 'feelings' as it is still something of an alien concept in the world of work. We are more used to talking about 'views' and 'opinions' and are therefore much more comfortable with these concepts. Working with feelings and emotions does not have to be any more complex than working with views and opinions. Feelings and emotions are just another way in which we as human beings express ourselves.

Project managers are sometimes concerned that when we talk about 'feelings and emotions' it will all get out of hand and end in tears. This should certainly not be the case if the situation is managed effectively and there are some basic rules that project managers can follow in order to avoid things getting out of hand.

A few pointers when working with feelings and emotions

- Encourage people to express how they feel in a non-personal way and to focus on the behaviours that people engage in as opposed to the person themselves; for example, instead of saying 'I hate Joan', say 'I hate the way that Joan refuses to respond to my requests until the last minute as this does not give me time to do what I need to do.'

- Agree a 'time out' signal during your first meeting when you are setting the ground rules. This is a gesture that you will all recognise, for example making a 'T' shape using both hands. This is a useful tool in that, if someone is expressing how they feel and they become too angry or too excited, you can use this gesture to indicate that they need to stop what they are saying and take a few minutes to cool down before they continue.

- If someone expresses how they feel and you do not know how to respond, just acknowledge what they have said by thanking them and ask if you can come back to it later. This gives you time to consider how best to respond. Another useful trick for buying some time if you do not know how to respond to something that has been said during a meeting is to ask anyone else present if they would like to comment on what has been said.

OPTIONS AND ALTERNATIVE STRATEGIES OR COURSES OF ACTION

By the time that you reach this stage, you should have explored and identified the root causes of the conflict and how all parties are feeling. This is the next stage where you progress to exploring what you can do to 'fix' the problem. Once again, as with the previous stage, there is no point in trying to rush things as you will lose the value of the process. Try not to offer solutions but instead encourage people to suggest solutions that they think will work for them. In this way, you are more likely to get real buy-in to whatever courses of action are agreed in order to resolve the conflict.

WHAT IS TO BE DONE, WHEN, BY WHOM, AND THE WILL TO DO IT

This is the final part of the 'GROW' model process and is about the practicalities of whatever action has been agreed. This is the stage at which you will agree the behavioural changes that individuals are going to make, that is, what they are going to do differently in order to avoid future conflict. Make sure that regular reviews are built into the action plan so you can monitor that change is taking place and that conflict is being reduced/avoided.

How Do You Use This Conflict Situation to Bring About New Knowledge and Team Development?

By working through the processes identified in the 'GROW' model, you will facilitate participants' self-learning as they explore how the behaviour of others makes them feel. In addition, they will learn more about the impact that their behaviour has on others. This learning should be harnessed through the process of asking participants to reflect on how they felt at the start of the process, how they felt during the process and how they feel at the end of the process. This reflection can then be used in one-to-one performance reviews and team development sessions.

Questions for Reflection

1. Thinking of situations in the past, have you generally avoided conflict or embraced it as a learning opportunity?

2. What monitoring measures will you put in place to ensure that you become aware of any signs of conflict at an early stage?

3. What strategies will you put in place to deal with any emerging conflict?

4. Are you confident that you currently have the skills to identify and deal with project conflict or do you need to further develop your repertoire of skills?

9

Project Management and Change Management

Modern-day projects can be complicated and vary from the small to the global; however, the vast majority of them will result in organisational change for some, if not all, groups within organisations. This means, in effect, that when you take on a project management role, you are taking on a change management role and any failure to acknowledge this is likely to result in the long-term failure of the project.

During the 90s in the UK, there were a significantly large number of projects around the introduction of new (computerised) technology in the UK. Burnes (1992) quotes a study carried out by A.T. Kearney which indicated that the UK was at the bottom of the league in terms of successful change management. The conclusion was that a third of all monies spent on introducing new technology (in the manufacturing sector) were wasted. This problem is not one that is specific to the UK alone, and other studies quoted by Burnes suggest that the failure rate of change projects involving technology is between 40 per cent and 70 per cent. These figures make for depressing reading and unfortunately the figures for other areas of project management are seldom much better.

The failure rate is rarely due to the technology not working but instead has more to do with the way in which the change is managed and implemented, which is where the project manager comes in.

I have experienced the implementation of a number of IT-related projects and the focus has always been on implementing the system with scarce attention paid to users and their needs, other than the offer of training after the implementation.

In my experience, many project managers focus on the project in a very linear way and follow critical paths in the hope that they will deliver the project. This can be a successful way to deliver a project, but the generally high failure rate of projects suggests that this is not enough, particularly where the objective of the project is to bring about a sustainable change. This suggests then that in order to be a good project manager, one also has to be a good change manager.

What Is Change Management?

Change can take many forms within organisations and varies in the impact that it has on the organisation and its constituent parts. Change can be viewed in terms of whether it is planned or emergent, that is, deliberately sought or naturally occurring; however, as we are only concerned with 'planned' change we need to analyse this a little further. Within academic circles, 'change' tends to be divided into two categories: incremental change and transformational change.

INCREMENTAL CHANGE

Incremental change, as the name suggests, tends of be of a more gradual nature and although it can be either planned or emergent, it is generally about the continuous enhancement of products or services. Some projects are about incremental change and these tend to be relatively small-scale and localised. The larger and more costly projects, however, tend to fall within the remit of 'transformational change' which tends to be perceived as the sexier side of change management.

TRANSFORMATIONAL CHANGE

This type of change tends to be more radical than incremental change and is often on a much larger scale. Transformational change is usually about organisation-wide projects that involve replacing old ways of working and thinking with new ones.

TRANSITIONAL CHANGE

Academics also now tend to use a third category to define change, which is 'transitional'. This type of change is transformational in nature but acknowledges that transformational change is often achieved through the delivery of smaller projects which move the organisation even further toward its planned state.

Managing Change within Projects

Managing change is not easy, but neither is it rocket science. A project manager who wants to deliver a successful project should produce a change management plan and incorporate it into his project plan. It is easy to assume that if you have produced a project plan, then you have produced a change plan; however, that is not usually the case. Project plans are usually about hard tasks that have to be delivered by certain people within certain timescales. They often do not take account of the highly charged emotional atmosphere that change can engender. There is a cliché which states that change is about hearts and minds, which is pretty much accurate. You can have the best project plan in the world but if you fail to manage the human side of change then your project is unlikely to succeed. There are additional benefits in carrying out 'people' diagnostics, in that you will also learn more about the organisational environment which will assist you with other areas of managing your project. When managing projects that involve significant change for people, it is helpful to have an understanding of some of the psychological processes that people undergo when faced with change.

PEOPLE RESPOND TO CHANGE IN DIFFERENT WAYS

As human beings, we are all different and we respond to different things in different ways and change situations are no different. Elizabeth Kubler-Ross (2005) suggested that people go through five stages of grief, when they are faced with a loss of some description, which could be experiencing a major change to their working environment, or losing their job or even suffering bereavement. The five stages are Denial, Anger, Bargaining, Depression and Acceptance.

Denial

This is the typical 'head in the sand' reaction that you often see when managing change. People convince themselves that it will not happen and tend to ignore communication about the change in the hope that it will go away. This denying of the truth can be conscious or unconscious, but either way it makes communication about the project particularly challenging and the project manager will have to ensure that he uses a variety of communication mediums and that the communication is consistent and persistent. This stage is a temporary self-defence mode that people go into when faced with change. This stage usually passes fairly quickly and is replaced by stage two, which is 'anger'.

Anger

Once people realise that 'denial' is no longer viable they may start to feel angry and aggrieved that the change is going to happen. You will hear comments like 'Everything is working fine, why change it?' or 'This sort of thing has been tried before, you know, it won't work. They are wasting their time.' Persistent and consistent communication through a range of media can be helpful in moving this stage along. The anger is often irrational and can be overwhelming in the short term. Individuals soon realise that they cannot maintain their anger indefinitely as colleagues who are more positive about the change become tired of them and management may start putting pressure on them to more effectively manage their emotions. This moves them on to the next stage which is 'bargaining'.

Bargaining

This is where the individual tries to do deals; for example, he may come up with a plan for his manager or team that involves working in a slightly different way as he thinks this may prevent the planned and communicated change from happening. If the individual's job or position is severely affected by the change, he may try to do a deal to retain his post or move to another area before the change commences. These types of bargaining initiatives rarely work, as by this point it is usually too late to prevent the change process as too much has already been invested. This then leads to the next stage, which is 'depression'.

Depression

This is where the individual is starting to realise that the change is going to go ahead anyway and that there is nothing that he can do personally to prevent it. The individual becomes low in mood at this time and may become socially withdrawn at work. He may appear to be quiet and distracted whilst showing little enthusiasm for anything. This stage is an important part of the 'grieving' process as it allows the individual to prepare himself or the next stage which is 'acceptance'.

Acceptance

At this stage, the individual starts to accept that the change will happen and that he might as well 'go with the flow'.

Not everyone goes through the above stages in the same order nor necessarily experiences all of the stages. Kubler-Ross suggests that some people will experience several stages in a 'roller coaster' effect; that is, they may toggle between several stages before returning to one. This model enables the project manager to have an understanding of the types of emotions that people are likely to be experiencing in response to his project. Project managers and other managers who are not aware of this model often interpret the emotions that they witness as 'resistance' and view them negatively as a problem to be resolved as opposed to a guide as to where to concentrate change efforts.

RESISTANCE TO CHANGE

The Kubler-Ross model shows us that we should anticipate resistance to change as it is part of the learning and adjustment process that individuals undergo in response to change situations. Remember though that the stages in the Kubler-Ross model are not about change per se but about situations of loss; that is, people will go through these stages when they think they are about to lose something or have lost something. In any change situation there are always people who perceive themselves as gaining something and people who perceive themselves as losing something. Obviously, the ones who see themselves as losing something are more likely to go through the stages described above. It is important to identify the potential 'losers' in any change project as this will enable you to anticipate any likely 'resistance'. Obviously, you will need to ensure that sufficient effort is put into working with this group in order to prevent any delays to or sabotage of your project.

DEALING WITH RESISTANCE

The key to dealing effectively with resistance to change is to understand the psychological processes that are going on and anticipate what is likely to happen at each stage of your project plan. In this way, you can build in the necessary support activities to ensure that people's fears are addressed and that the required change is supported. There are some diagnostic tools listed later on in this chapter which will help you produce an effective change plan.

READINESS TO CHANGE

There is a second psychological process associated with change management which is called 'readiness to change'. This process describes a person's emotional readiness to change. In the previous section, we talked about people who perceive themselves as losing something as a result of the change process undergoing five phases of emotional adjustment. It is important to recognise, however, that each person will have a different 'readiness to change' or 'tipping' point which means that you cannot assume that those people included in the change process who do not perceive a loss will change exactly when you need them to. 'Readiness to change' is about the motivation of the individual to change, it is about their decision-making processes and their wider emotions and cognitions.

Prochaska and DiClemente (1986) suggested that there are five stages that individuals go through in order to change:

1. pre-contemplation

2. contemplation

3. preparation

4. action

5. maintenance

Pre-contemplation

At this stage, the individual has no plans to change. This may be because he is unaware of the change, that is, the communication about change has not reached him or he has not understood it. Alternatively, he could be in Kubler-Ross's denial stage. This individual may appear to be resisting change.

Contemplation

In this stage, the individual is now more aware of the change and what it involves. At this point, the individual will be weighing up the pros and cons of the change to work out what they are likely to gain or lose. Prochaska and DiClemente suggest that this balancing of advantages and disadvantages can be quite confusing and a little overwhelming sometimes. This can lead to individuals being stuck in this stage for several months. Prochaska and DiClemente refer to these individuals as being 'Behavioural Procrastinators'.

Preparation

This is where people are preparing to change and may have already worked out exactly how they need to go about it and have an action plan for what to do.

Action

This is the stage where the individual has started to change his behaviour and or attitudes. The 'Action' stage is also the critical stage where vigilance is needed to ensure that the individual does not relapse into old behaviours and attitudes.

Maintenance

This is the stage where people have reached a new equilibrium (see Lewin's 'Refreezing' stage below). At this stage, the new behaviours have become the norm and people are less tempted to relapse into their old ways of thinking and doing things. This stage has something in common with Kubler-Ross's 'Acceptance' phase.

The above stages are generally the stages that individuals undergo in order to decide that they are going to change and as with the Kubler-Ross model; people will vary in the speed at which they work through the stages. Basically, the model proposed by Prochaska and DiClemente illustrates that individuals will only change when they are psychologically and emotionally ready to do so. The responsibility of the project manager is to facilitate this psychological and emotional readiness as much as possible by taking the concept of 'Readiness to Change' into account when planning for change and putting processes in place to help ensure that people:

- understand the change and its implications for them

- feel engaged in the change, that is, feel that they have a real say in it

- feel that there is sufficient openness, honesty and transparency to feel that they can trust the agents of change

- feel that they have something to gain from it

- feel supported and that someone is on their side and is looking out for them

What Do I Need to Do in Order to Produce a Change Management Plan?

You will need to look closely at what the project is trying to achieve and who will be most affected by it. Find out what the change means to them and how they feel about it. You will need to go beyond the rational thinking level of what the change means for them and explore the degree of emotional attachment that they have to the current ways of working and thinking, which will be changed by your project. In order to obtain this deeper level of understanding about the impact of your project, you will need to carry out some diagnostics.

WHAT DIAGNOSTIC TOOLS CAN I USE?

There are many models of change which vary in their complexity and usefulness; however, a good diagnostic tool to start with is the 'field of forces' model developed by Kurt Lewin (in Burnes 1992). Although this is an old model, it has stood the test of time and is still a useful starting point in the management of any change project. The model is from what is known as the 'group dynamics school' which emphasises bringing about organisational change through teams or work groups rather than individuals. Lewin viewed group behaviour as a set of structures which modify the behaviour not only of groups but also of the individuals who make up those groups. From this perspective, then, the easiest way to target individual behaviour is by manipulating the norms, roles and values of organisational teams and groups. Do remember that although you will be targeting work groups with your change interventions, the individual psychological processes that we discussed earlier in the chapter will be generating a potential hotbed of emotions which you will need to take account of and work with. When trying to achieve change, you will generally be using the levers of norms, rules and values.

NORMS

These are the rules that guide how team members should act and think in response to certain situations; for example, be friendly and helpful to new members of the team.

RULES

These are the expectations that organisations have of people in different roles which are sometimes about the formal role description associated with the job but are often influenced by other factors such as norms that have evolved over time around the various roles and sometimes the values of the organisation/ team/individual.

VALUES

These are the collective beliefs that people within a team or organisation hold about what is right or wrong.

Lewin's Field of Forces Analysis

Lewin's Field of Forces states that in any change project, there will be drivers towards making the change happen and drivers towards preventing the change from happening. If the two sets of drivers are equally strong, then no progress will be made in bringing about change. This means that if you are serious about making change happen, you will have to ensure that the driving forces for change are strong enough to overcome any resistance and inertia.

The driving forces for change can be many and varied:

- a need to compete more effectively in a particular market

- technology becoming out of date

- diversification

- preparing for the future

The drivers against change can also be varied:

- group or individual resistance

- organisational inertia

- a lack of understanding/knowledge about the change

- insufficient mechanisms to bring about change

Figure 9.1   Lewin's field of forces

In order to understand and manage change, you really know what these opposing forces are so that you can plan to either reduce the forces against change or increase the forces for change; depending on which course of action is likely to be most successful. Sometimes it is necessary to work on both simultaneously.

Carrying out this type of diagnostic will also help provide an additional dimension of understanding to your stakeholder analysis as it will demonstrate:

- where the balance of power lies

- which stakeholders are likely to be your allies and which of them may be opponents

- where you need to invest the bulk of your energies

In carrying out this diagnostic, you will need to take the time to get close to people and to ask the right questions in order to gauge a feel for the strength of feeling and emotional attachment that people have. This information will guide you with regard to what levers you could use in order to make your project successful. You will benefit from adopting a 'coaching' approach and asking people not only what they think about the forthcoming change but also how they feel about it. Once you have completed this diagnostic, you should be fairly, if not totally, clear about the behaviours and attitudes that exist amongst your other stakeholders and whose work is most impacted by your project.

LEWIN'S THREE STAGES FOR BRINGING ABOUT CHANGE

Kurt Lewin also introduced another diagnostic tool which is very useful for project managers whose projects involve change. Basically, Lewin suggested that in order to make change happen you have to go through three phases:

1.   unfreezing

2.   moving

3.   refreezing

Unfreezing

The first stage, 'unfreezing', assumes that people are 'stuck' or 'frozen' into certain routine behaviours or attitudes and that one of the first steps of any change process must be about making people realise that they need to change. Addressing this phase of change is likely to take a significant amount of effort. A number of activities may be necessary in order to make this happen – for example, persuasive communication around why the change is necessary. It may also be necessary at this stage to provide training in any new ways of working so that people are able to view or do things differently. Team building exercises and/or management development activities can also be extremely effective at this stage. The aim is to get people ready for change both practically and mentally. We will go on to look at some diagnostic tools to achieve this, later on in this chapter.

Moving

This phase is about actually learning from the first phase and implementing the planned changes, that is, people behaving in appropriate ways and demonstrating the attitudes required for the new regime. At this stage, support will be needed to help the change which may involve training and reinforcement of changed behaviours and attitudes. From a psychological perspective, this is very much a transitional stage for those people involved in the change. It is where they dip their toes in the water to see how hot it is and how different it feels. Some people are likely to be a little sensitive and fearful at this stage and will need encouragement to progress.

Refreezing

This final phase of change is about ensuring that the new equilibrium that has been reached is maintained and that people do not slip back into the old ways of thinking and behaving. In this phase you are trying to make the changed behaviours and attitudes permanent so that they become the accepted way of thinking and behaving. Support mechanisms needed at this stage are likely to be reinforcement of the new behaviours/attitudes. Strong communication is likely to be needed in support of the new behaviours and attitudes. In addition, organisational structures and processes should be changed where necessary to ensure that everything is aligned in support of the new 'norm'.

One of the benefits of this three-phase model is that it emphasises that for human beings change is a psychological journey with many twists and turns as opposed to a direct route to a different way of working. It also recognises the concept of change readiness, which is often ignored in project management and it emphasises the need to provide appropriate support at each stage of the journey. Once you have identified what needs to happen at each of the three stages, these activities can be incorporated into your project plan. You will need to work closely with key stakeholders and the senior team to ensure that they understand the change management activities that you will need them to take responsibility for and deliver in order to make the project a success. When producing your change plan, there may be some things that you cannot influence, for example, leadership and organisational structures. These obstacles should be included in feedback to your project board and they should also feature in your risk analysis.

It is worth mentioning that projects will differ considerably in the extent and depth of behavioural change required. For some projects, the behavioural changes required may be fairly limited, for example someone having to go and work in a different team or department. Equally for other projects, significant behavioural changes may be necessary. Huse (1980 in Burnes 1992) suggested that change interventions can be categorised into a continuum of four levels:

- the shallow level

- the deep level

- the deeper level

- the deepest level

Huse maintained that 'the greater the depth of the intervention the more it becomes concerned with the psychological make-up and personality of the individual and the greater the need for full involvement of the individual if they are to accept the changes'. The 'shallow' level is about structural and technical changes, for example, reducing from five levels of management to four levels of management. The 'deep' level is about change activities where the individual has to reflect on his own behaviour, for example, changes to roles and job descriptions. The 'deeper' level of change is about situations where the individual has to reflect on aspects of his personality and how he relates to people, for example, team building and process consultation. The 'deepest' level refers to change initiatives that force individuals to consider their life choices and fundamental aspects of their personality, for example, career planning/outsourcing. The change continuum suggested by Huse implies that the extent to which stakeholders are involved in the change process increases as you move down the continuum. In other words, the bigger the impact of change on the individual as a person, the more effort needs to be put into engaging them and gaining their buy-in.

HOW DO YOU BRING ABOUT CHANGE?

There are three ways in which you can bring about change, using Lewin's Field of Forces. You can increase the forces that are pushing for change, you can decrease the forces against change or you can influence both sets of forces at the same time. You will need to use emotional leverage to increase or decrease the forces alongside any practical measures. Once you have gone through the diagnostic phase identified above, you should have sufficient understanding of the various drivers and consequently be able to start influencing them. Remember that you cannot bring about change on your own and your role will be about harnessing the energies of those who can help, that is, the stakeholders and senior managers in the organisation who may or may not be involved in the project. You will have to ensure that the people you involve in the change process are very clear about what change you need to achieve and what their role in the process should be.

There are a number of tools that you can use in order to ensure that the changes you are implementing are sustainable in the long term. One of the most important tools is communication, which we described in Chapter 6; however, there are other tools which are equally valuable, which are described shortly.

Creating Sustainable Change

How do you make sure that the changes you are implementing are sustainable? There are a number of factors that are important when trying to create sustainable change:

- planning

- clarity about the nature and direction of the change process

- a review of organisational policies and processes

- a review of reward strategies

- communication

- training

- monitoring and review

- management/leadership

PLANNING

The crucial aspect of making any change sustainable is the planning process. When planning the change, build in the factors that will sustain it and stop people slipping back into the old behaviours. You will need to ensure that mechanisms are in place to maintain the drivers for change and ensure that they remain stronger than the forces against them. In other words, you will need a clearly delineated plan to manage the transition from project to steady state. If you are an external project manager or someone borrowed from a different department, you will not be around to ensure that the changes are sustained, and if this is the case you will need to ensure that you identify suitable people in your plan who will be around to ensure that the changes continue beyond the life of the project.

CLARITY AROUND THE CHANGE PROCESS

Ensure that everyone is clear about what the change is trying to achieve and why. People are more likely to continue supporting the change process if they can understand it and see what it is trying to achieve.

REVIEW ORGANISATIONAL POLICIES AND PROCESSES

Review organisational polices and processes to ensure that they all push in favour of the change.

REVIEW REWARD STRATEGIES

It may be necessary also to review reward and appraisal polices to ensure that they are all aligned in support of the change process.

COMMUNICATION

Communication is not only important throughout the project phases, it is also very important when the project phase ends. There will be a need for some ongoing communication at the end of the project that informs people of what the project has achieved but also spells out what more is expected of people in order to maintain the changes.

TRAINING

In addition, you will need to ensure that people have the skills, knowledge and tools that they need to deliver the new behaviours that are expected of them. I have witnessed a number of change processes where the organisations involved have waited until the end of the change process before offering any training. It can often be helpful to provide training much earlier in the process so that people have more clarity about what to expect in the future. This can help alleviate some of the fear and also gives employees an opportunity to start changing attitudes and behaviours early on in the process. This may result in a need for ongoing training or refresher training at appropriate intervals, including after the project phases have ended.

MONITORING AND REVIEW

In the same way that progress against change was measured during the project phases, it will also need to monitored and reviewed on an ongoing basis. In my experience, once a project ends, everyone assumes that the change is in place and that it will continue. Sometimes this is true, but often, unfortunately, it is not and once the support and monitoring is withdrawn, the change is replaced by old habits and fails. There are advantages to continuing to monitor change in that, firstly, if anything is going off track, it can be quickly remedied. Secondly, the very act of monitoring progress can be used as a method of achieving continuous improvement.

LEADERSHIP/MANAGEMENT SUPPORT

In order for the changed processes to be sustained, it will be necessary for managers to demonstrate continued support for them even after the project phase has ended. The project manager will need to ensure that managers are clear about the types of actions that they will need to take after the project has ended and that they have a plan to achieve this. Leaders will need also need to demonstrate their support for the new processes and will need to ensure that they act as role models and ambassadors for them.

A WORD OF CAUTION

A slight word of caution is necessary with regard to splitting and rearranging teams. Research from 'Gallup' on staff engagement indicates that one of the contributory factors to being engaged with the organisation is about 'having a friend' at work. For some people, that friend will be a team member, so do not split teams up unless it is absolutely necessary. Changing teams also provides an additional layer of stress and uncertainty for team members.

Questions for Reflection

1. Does your project plan include a plan for bringing about sustainable change?

2.   Are you aware of existing organisational forces that could either drive or derail your project?

3.   Have you identified which categories of organisational members view themselves as the winners and losers regarding the changes that will be brought about by your project?

4.   Do you have a strategy for taking the emotional temperature of the organisation and successfully addressing resistance to change and high levels of emotion?

5.   How will you assess the organisation's 'readiness for change'?

6.   Do you have a strategy to support the various phases of change?

7.   How will you evaluate the progress of change?

8.   How will you ensure that the change is sustainable beyond the life of the project?

10

Using Your Project Board

The Project Board

Project boards are sometimes assembled before the project manager is recruited which means that the new project manager is faced with a fait accompli. On other occasions, the project manager is appointed first and has the happy task of choosing his own project board members. Having experienced both scenarios, I am not sure which position is actually the best one for a project manager to be in. Each situation has its own relative merits and disadvantages.

Choosing a Project Board

Choosing project board members can be a bit of a nightmare and it is important to put some thought into the task before jumping in with both feet. There are a number of considerations when choosing a project board; for example, how many people should you have on the project board, which elements of the business should be represented on the project board? Given that the project board is going to be a decision-making and advisory body, it is probably worth keeping the membership as small as possible. When starting projects, there is often a temptation to ensure that every stakeholder is represented on the project board. This is not necessary, however, and research has demonstrated that larger project boards tend to have less clarity about roles which leads to low attendance and, we can assume, poor engagement, thus making them more inefficient. Remember that the function of the project board is to lead the project and there are many alternative ways of engaging with your stakeholders. If you are recruited into a project management role with an existing board like this, you would be advised to ask for a review of the membership.

A second consideration is around the level of responsibility and decision-making power that the board has. The 'Office of Government and Commerce'

(OGC) suggests that the 'senior responsible officer' or project owner should retain responsibility for decision-making with the board acting as an advisory body.

Common Problems with Project Boards

In the introduction to this book, we talked about why projects fail, and unfortunately project boards have to share some of the responsibility for this failure. Every project manager will have stories to tell about poorly functioning project boards. The list below highlights some of the key failings of project boards.

1.   Lack of sufficient challenge.

2.   Low attendance.

3.   Low engagement.

4.   Confrontational relationships.

5.   Differential agendas.

6.   Hijacking agendas.

7.   Failure to act as an ambassador for the project.

8.   Failure to take appropriate and timely decisions.

LACK OF SUFFICIENT CHALLENGE

Time and time again, project managers tell me that the board was not sufficiently challenging. Sometimes the lack of challenge is in reference to the project itself. On other occasions, the lack of challenge is around the project board failing to adequately challenge itself as a project board.

What can the project manager do to encourage challenge?

Challenge can often be quite uncomfortable for you as a project manager because it can often feel as though you are the one in the firing line and you are being asked to justify your actions. Challenge is a necessary evil, however, and helps project managers and project boards ensure that they are making the right decision or even if they are going in the right direction. It also avoids the type of 'groupthink' that we talked about in Chapter 3, whereby everyone goes along with a decision without challenging it.

What you don't want as project manager is a situation where all the challenge is about your actions within the project. This can feel a little like being on trial and does not generally create good working relationships between you and your project board. It is important to create the right kind of atmosphere where there is trust and where project board members feel comfortable in expressing concerns and challenging decisions. Unfortunately, this will not always be under your control and if you have joined a project with a ready-made project board, then you may have little influence over the personalities on the board. This does not mean, however, that you cannot influence the degree of challenge. By creating strong relationships with each of your project board members, you will be able to attain more of a feel for what they really think about where the project is going. This will help you to feel more comfortable with the board members as individuals and more confident in encouraging them to challenge the project and its objectives.

Project board members can sometimes be very senior and difficult to access but it is worth persevering and discussing moot points with them prior to the project board meeting. It will also help if you prepare some questions before the project board meeting that you can use to facilitate challenge. For example:

Given the various changes in the business, are you still confident that we are heading in the right direction?

Are there any other strategies that we should be considering?

These questions are only simplistic examples but you can see that they are simply prompts designed to challenge people's thinking and to encourage them to think more broadly. You can also encourage your project board to challenge more by providing them with more feedback about the impact that certain aspects of the project may have had, either positively or negatively. This will help the project board to gain more of an understanding of how the project is being received and, once again, may encourage them to think more widely about the project.

How can the project board encourage itself to challenge more?

There are actions that the project board itself can take to ensure that it offers an appropriate level of challenge. One such step is the agreeing of ground rules. This can be very helpful when you have very senior people on the project board as less senior people can be afraid of speaking or challenging. It would be sensible for project boards to set some basic guidelines around everyone having an equal say in discussions (as long as someone accepts responsibility for making the final decision) and everyone's input being sought. In addition, there should be guidelines around respecting other people's views and exploring them, that is, not just listening to them and dismissing them out of hand. This will ensure that everyone manages to voice their opinion, which is more likely to lead to challenge and an appropriate decision at the end of the day. Project boards could also nominate one member to act as 'devil's advocate' and challenge at regular intervals just to prompt discussion. This is a little extreme but it has been used to good effect by some groups where there is no one who is willing to offer challenge.

LOW ATTENDANCE

Poor attendance tends to be more common in certain kinds of project board, as we said earlier in this chapter; the larger project boards are more prone to poor attendance as are those who are involved in poorly managed projects and/or where roles and responsibilities are unclear.

Low attendance can be very disruptive and demoralising to a project manager, disruptive in that decisions may have to be deferred until the absent board member is able to comment. It can also be demoralising when only half your project board bothers to attend meetings and can send a message that the project is not important, which can discourage other project board members from attending.

What can you do to encourage good attendance at project board meetings?

Firstly, you can ensure that your project is well managed and that the project board members are clear about what you need from them. You can also encourage good attendance by contacting non-attendees and giving them the impression that they were missed – assuming that you have the time. Perhaps the most useful strategy however, is to enlist the help of the chair to put pressure on people to attend. Project board members will have been selected because they are key stakeholders or because they have a particular expertise or experience that they can offer to the project. If they fail to attend project board meetings, the project is losing something potentially valuable which could increase the risk. Ultimately, if a project board member is not able or willing to attend meetings regularly, it is worth considering a replacement.

LOW ENGAGEMENT

Low engagement is something else that a lot of project managers complain about. You often hear comment such as 'they don't read the papers before the project board meetings' or 'they ask the same question at every meeting'.

What can you do to avoid low engagement?

Low engagement is a particularly tricky problem to address because it does not matter how much effort you put in, if someone does not wish to engage then they will not do so. Hopefully, few of your project board members will fall into this category and there are things that you can do to promote engagement. In Chapter 5 we talked about engaging stakeholders and the same principles apply to engaging project board members. You will need to ensure that you build a relationship with them as we discussed earlier in this chapter and that you ensure that they feel as involved as possible in the project. The key is around 'building shared ownership', which means that your project board members will feel that they have some personal responsibility for the project.

You will need to ensure that your project reporting brings the project to life for them and captivates their interest. Where possible, use stories and anecdotes from your experience of delivering the project. In addition, try to make your project board members feel valued, ask their opinions, and make contact with them outside project board meetings. We will go on later in this chapter to talk about 'using your project board as a resource'.

CONFRONTATIONAL RELATIONSHIPS

A number of unlucky project managers find themselves working to project boards where their relationship is adversarial and they feel as though they are 'under fire' at every meeting. This appears to be a common experience when you speak to project managers.

How can you avoid confrontational relationships?

We looked at confrontation and how to deal with it in Chapter 9 and there are a number of techniques and strategies that you can employ to reduce conflict. We have talked repeatedly in this chapter about the importance of building good relationships with your project board and this really is the key to avoiding adversarial relationships with your project board. If, however, you find yourself in this situation then I would recommend that you reflect on what has changed or how you have reached that situation; for example, is it that the project board disagrees with an approach that you are taking or is it more deep rooted than that? Conflict can occur when people feel threatened, that is, they become defensive and possibly hostile. By reflecting on the project board meetings that felt adversarial, you will quickly reach a conclusion about which members were particularly hostile and you will start to formulate some theories around why this might be. It may be the case that you have to take the time to meet certain members individually in order to better understand where they are coming from and alleviate their fears.

DIFFERENTIAL AGENDAS

I have heard of occasions where project board members had different agendas, sometimes because the members misunderstood what the project was trying to achieve or where they had not been appropriately briefed about the project.

What can you do to try and ensure that everyone is singing from the same hymn sheet?

The first thing that you can do is to ensure that there is as much clarity as possible about what the project is trying to achieve. It may be necessary to keep reiterating this at the start of project meetings. Remember, project board members will have day jobs as well and reiterating the mission of the project at the start of the meeting can be a good way of focusing people on the project.

If you find yourself in a situation where some project board members clearly have different agendas then clarifying the mission for the project is unlikely to have much of an impact. In situations like these, you will need to try and understand what the different agenda is about. Occasionally, project members find themselves battling for power, and subtle sabotage can creep in. Once again, in these situations, it is often better to talk to the individuals concerned outside the meeting (assuming your comments within the meeting have fallen on deaf ears) and try to achieve two things. First of all, you need to understand why the individual appears to be suggesting or doing things that are not consistent with the requirements of the project, as it is only by understanding the motives of the individual that you will understand why they are behaving in the way that they are. Secondly, it provides you with an opportunity to explain what the project needs to achieve and to explore if there is any way for the person's agenda to be met whilst maintaining the direction of the project plan.

The 'coaching' approaches that we looked at in Chapter 4 will assist you in gaining a better understanding of what you are dealing with. If you are unable to convince the project board member(s) that their suggested or actual actions are not in the best interests of the project, you will have to have a quiet word with the project board chair/project owner and see if they can assist you in bringing the wayward project board member back in line.

HIJACKING AGENDAS

It is not uncommon within project boards to find members who try to hijack the agenda and bend it to their own particular requirements. Often these are individuals who are not wholly in agreement with the project. Alternatively, someone may hijack an agenda to get a better deal for their department.

This type of situation is very similar to the 'different agendas' scenario described above. The only difference is that in this situation, the project board member is not introducing his or her own agenda. He is instead trying to use the agenda to achieve something for himself.

How can you deal with agenda hijackers?

The way of dealing with this scenario is the same as when dealing with project board members who have different agendas. The key, once again, is about understanding what is motivating the project board member and then looking at whether you can arrive at a 'win/win' situation. In addition, you can utilise some of the communication techniques that we looked at in Chapter 6 to help keep people focused on what you and the project need to achieve.

FAILURE TO ACT AS AN AMBASSADOR TO THE PROJECT

I have heard many project managers bemoan the fact that project board members have failed to share project information with their areas of the organisation or promote the project in any shape or form.

How can you encourage your project board members to act as ambassadors to the project?

I have come to the conclusion that project board members generally see their role as attending project board meetings and ensuring that the project is steered in the right direction. I think that the concept of being an ambassador for the project with their own and other departments tends to fall by the wayside. I think this probably happens for a number of reasons. Firstly, everyone is busy these days and people often have more on their plates than they can actually achieve so they actually just don't get round to it. Secondly, I do not think that project boards are always clear that this duty is expected of them. Thirdly, I do not think that some project boards know what it is they should be doing to act as an ambassador to the project.

This means that there are a number of potential actions that you can take. Firstly, when you agree the terms of reference for your project board, make sure that there is a sentence in there that specifies that they will need to act as ambassadors to the project. Secondly, you need to specify exactly what you need your project board to do, in terms of being ambassadors; for example, do you need to them to 'sell' the project to their own departments, or do you need them to 'sell' the project to the organisation? You will need to be very clear about where you want them to act as ambassadors. In addition, you may need to suggest some specific actions to them, for example holding meetings with their own departmental managers to feed back specific points from the project and elicit views. The bottom line is that the more specific you can be about the types of behaviours that you require, the easier it will be for the project board to understand their responsibilities. In addition, once you have identified the behaviours required, you can review progress made at each project board meeting. This has the additional benefit of keeping the required behaviours firmly in the mind of your project board. If you are recruited into a situation where the board already have terms of reference, you can always suggest that they are reviewed so that you can include any requirements to act as an ambassador. We talked about engagement in Chapter 5 and helping to create an atmosphere of shared ownership. This will also help you to make the project board feel part of the project on an ongoing basis.

FAILURE TO TAKE DECISIONS

Many project boards find themselves in the position of being faced with some very difficult project decisions, some of which could be very costly or damaging if the wrong decision is made. The better project boards are able to rely on their project information and risk management data to have an objective discussion that informs the correct decision to take. Unfortunately, not all project boards function this way. Some project boards have poor risk management information that fails to help them in reaching a decision. Other project boards may have high-quality risk management information but are either risk aversive and unable to make a timely decision or are unable to have the type of quality debate that would arrive at the optimum decision to take.

How can you ensure that your project boards make the right decision?

You are unlikely to be in a position to replace a project board that is unable to make decisions or which makes risk-averse decisions but there are probably several actions that you can take to help your board arrive at the right decisions. Firstly, you can ensure that you provide your project board with sufficient information for them to make a decision. Some project boards will feel comfortable with minimal information and others will require something more substantial in order to make a decision. You will need to get become familiar with the approach that your board takes to decision-making so that you can develop a strategy to ensure that you get the decisions that you need in a timely manner. You will also have to ensure that you provide sufficient information regarding the risks associated with various decisions and, once again, every project board is different with regard to the amount of information on risks that it needs in order to make a decision. If you experience a situation where the project board is struggling to reach a decision, ask them what more you could have provided to make the decision easier.

Sometimes project boards struggle to make decisions for reasons that are not related to the amount or nature of information that they receive; sometimes it is because the decision is particularly difficult, or more commonly because they are not very good as a group at reaching decisions. This is a particularly difficult situation and your ability to influence this situation will depend very much on the nature of your relationship with the project board. If you have a project board that has poor group processes and you see them committing some of the 'team process' errors such as 'groupthink' that we discussed in Chapter 3, then the best thing that you can do is arrange for training for your project board members to help them become more effective. Obviously, this is unlikely to happen in cash-strapped organisations or where the project is relatively short-lived; however, for larger or more expensive projects, a small investment in training the project board could reap massive dividends.

If your project board are unlikely to be receptive to the idea of training, then you could suggest that they allocate 30 minutes or so to the of each project board meeting to review how they operated as a project board and what worked well and what did not. Ideally, you would have someone neutral from outside the project board facilitating this, perhaps someone from your HR department or an external consultant if sufficient funds are available.

How to Protect Yourself as a Project Manager When Others Fail to Cooperate

If you spend 10 minutes talking to any project manager in the UK (or probably across the globe for that matter), they will tell you horror stories of where projects have gone wrong and they were worried about facing the project board. With the best will in the world, there will always be the odd surprise when delivering projects, that is, the curve ball that comes out of nowhere. If you ignore these little tricks that life plays on us, most situations where projects go wrong are foreseeable and often the project manager can see the early signs that all is not going well. Unfortunately, a number of project managers look to hide these early warnings and pretend that all is going well. This is a big mistake. The project board is there to help keep the project on track and oversee its direction. They are not there solely to hear good news stories. You should treat the project board as a personal resource for you. After all, they are there to support you not to castigate and punish you.

USING YOUR PROJECT BOARD AS A RESOURCE

If you can see the signs that something is not going to go as planned then share it with your project board along with the reasons as to why it is not going well. They may be able to help you, particularly where the problem is occurring as a result of a senior stakeholder not delivering their part of the plan. Even if they are unable to help you, it is better to keep them informed of both good and bad news. Project managers often feel that it reflects badly on their performance if they share bad news; however, the project board is there to be utilised and you should call on their knowledge and expertise to help you deal with project difficulties that arise. It sometimes appears as though there is an 'us and them' culture between the project manager and the project board, but it does not have to be like this. A sensible project manager will build a good relationship with his project board and help create a trusting and supportive atmosphere where people can talk about issues in a constructive and helpful way without feeling the need to apportion blame.

Questions for Reflection

1. Are you sufficiently clear about what you need from your project board and have you communicated this to them?

2. Is your project board an optimum size and do you have a plan to engage its members?

3. Do you feel that your project board is operating at an effective level in terms of their decision-making and level of risk taking?

4. Do you trust your project board and do you feel that they have trust in you?

5. Are you able to be open and honest with your project board, or do you feel that you have to 'sugar-coat' bad news?

11

Do Organisations Learn From Failed Projects?

Do Organisations Learn From Failed Projects?

From the relatively high percentage of failed projects, it would appear that a large number of organisations do not learn from their failures, or at least do not learn enough from their failures to prevent reoccurrences. Papastamatiou (2005) provides an example of an 'energy' company that repeatedly failed to deliver its projects successfully as a result of failing to learn from its mistakes. Mark Keil (1999) has experience of numerous IT based projects and he comments that 'then when these projects fail there is seldom any effort to systematically learn from that failure; instead the whole episode is swept under the rug'. Kharbanda and Stallworthy (1983) comment that 'Man is so obsessed with his need to succeed that project disasters are usually just filed away. The management literature is replete with success stories, but hardly any attention is paid to failures, let alone to the lessons they could teach us.' Given the potentially high costs of failure and the potential embarrassment of senior teams explaining reduced dividends to shareholders, it is not surprising perhaps that people sometimes prefer to hide failure as opposed to exploring it.

Why Should Organisations Learn From Failed Projects?

Not learning from failure is a bit of a no-brainer because if you do not learn from your mistakes, you are likely to carry on repeating them ad infinitum. In addition we can often learn far more from our failures than from our successes. Ackoff (1994) comments that:

> When one does something right one only confirms what is already known: how to do it. A mistake is an indicator of a gap in one's

knowledge. Learning takes place when a mistake is identified, its producers are identified and it is corrected.

Many modern business theorists suggest that the best competitive edge that a company can have is the ability to learn quickly and adapt. In addition, as we have said repeatedly, failed projects can be very costly not only in delivery costs but also in the damage that can occur to brands and customer loyalty when things go wrong. Consequently, it is in the best commercial interest of every organisation to ensure that it learns from its mistakes and encourages people to speak up when things are not going well so that the reasons can be explored and understood.

THE PROJECT ENVIRONMENT – DOES IT PUNISH FAILURE?

The extent to which people feel able to admit to mistakes in an organisation depends on a number of factors – for example, the organisational culture, type of leadership, attitude of immediate manager, the seniority of the person who makes a mistake, the consequences of the mistake for self, consequences of the mistake for others, and so on. Organisational culture is probably the most crucial influence on whether or not people feel comfortable admitting to mistakes and/or failures. Some organisations encourage people to be honest and open about mistakes and to learn from them, whereas other organisations can have very punitive cultures where, the moment a mistake comes to light, a witch hunt is launched immediately in order to find a scapegoat to blame it on. Understandably, people in the latter type of organisation are less likely to admit to making a mistake than people in the first type of organisation. We will go on later in this chapter to look at organisational learning and what measures organisations need to put in place in order to be able to learn from project failures.

ORGANISATIONAL DEFENSIVE ROUTINES

Argrys and Schon (1996) suggests that organisations develop defensive routines in order to avoid the potential embarrassment of failed projects or things not working well. These defensive routines can take many forms, from communicating in a vague and general manner so that other organisational members cannot understand what is being communicated, let alone ask any awkward questions, to accepting 'common' knowledge at face value and failing to challenge anything. This is a little like the 'groupthink' phenomena that we looked at in Chapter 3 but on a grander scale. Argrys comments that 'Defensive routines are systemic, in that most people within the company adhere to them. People leave the organisation and new ones arrive but the defensive routines remain intact.'

All organisations utilise defensive routines to some degree but they will be more prevalent in organisations where there is a lower level of trust and/or a punitive culture. These defensive routines tend to work reasonably well in avoiding difficult questions and any suggestion that all is not working as well as it could do. Unfortunately, these routines are not very good for organisational learning as they prevent people from exploring why something has or has not worked and thus prevent people from benefiting from that experience. Argrys refers to these defensive routines as 'self-sealing loops' which I think paints a really good mental picture of why learning does not take place when these defensive routines are utilised.

'EXPLICIT' AND 'TACIT' KNOWLEDGE

Tanaka (1996) suggests that there are two kinds of knowledge: 'explicit' knowledge and 'tacit' knowledge. 'Explicit' knowledge is the type that is often formally documented, for example, the instructions for using your TV. This type of knowledge can easily be communicated. 'Tacit' knowledge, on the other hand, is the type that is particular to an individual based on his or her experience, for example, the type of knowledge that a master baker has in order to produce a perfect loaf every time he bakes. Tanaka (1996) suggests that 'tacit' knowledge is a combination of technical know-how which is generally gained through experience and various beliefs, mental models and perspectives. It is important to recognise that 'tacit' information can exist not just in an individual but in a set of relationships, for example a working group established to complete a particular task. 'Explicit' information is usually well captured in organisations, for example in operating manuals and work processes. It is also often the type of knowledge that is stored in shared electronic systems in intranets throughout numerous companies. The more difficult information to gather and interpret is the 'tacit' knowledge that exists in project members heads and other members of the organisation.

Organisations often invest large sums of money on intranet sites to manage knowledge but they may not be capturing the best knowledge. Essentially, learning is about making sense of something and a body of knowledge similar to that contained in a typical knowledge management website is less useful than knowledge of the processes needed to continually revise or update that knowledge. In order to harness those processes, it is necessary for organisations to implement some fundamental organisational learning processes.

WHAT IS ORGANISATIONAL LEARNING?

Learning occurs in all organisations even when there are no processes to facilitate or support that learning. This is known as 'accidental learning' and although it is helpful and may lead to better organisational practices or the production of better products. Unfortunately, without processes to document and share the learning appropriately, the experience is unlikely to achieve the potential impact that it could have. In order to understand learning per se and how organisational learning takes place, it is useful to look at Kolb's experiential learning model.

For Kolb, learning is a four-stage process that starts with concrete experience and reflecting on this experience. This reflection and observation generate new theories which are then tested out to create new experiences which are then observed and reflected on. Thus the cycle continues. Kolb's model divides learners into four different categories according to the way in which they prefer to learn and there is a questionnaire that people can complete which identifies their particular learning styles. Awareness of our own individual learning style helps improve both individual and organisational learning so it is important to be aware of the Kolb learning cycle and our own particular learning styles. Unfortunately, this in itself is not enough to facilitate organisational learning.

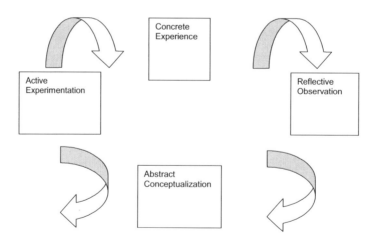

Figure 11.1   Kolb's experiential learning model (Kolb 1984)

Kolb's model was originally designed as a way of understanding the way in which individuals learn; however, it can also be applied to help understand how organisations learn. By encouraging individual members to learn, an organisation can improve processes and practices but only in a limited way. In order for organisational learning to take place, a number of additional mechanisms need to be put in place. Organisational learning should be an explicit objective and it will not happen in any sustainable way unless time is invested in developing processes and procedures to implement it.

Organisations need to engage in the same four stages of the learning cycle if they are to learn from their experiences; however, Dixon (1994) suggests that organisations need to facilitate collective learning and they can achieve this by implementing four additional mechanisms to support the learning cycle and extend it to facilitate the type of collaborative learning needed within an organisation:

1. The widespread generation of information.

2. The integration of new information into the organisational context.

3. The collective interpretation of information.

4. Empowering staff to take responsible action based on the interpreted meaning.

Each individual within the organisation must undergo all stages within the learning cycle if learning is to take place, but for organisational learning to take place, all members of the organisation must experience the learning cycle and somehow a mechanism must be developed to harness the experiences, observations and reflections (*the widespread generation of information*). Once this information has been collected, someone has to assimilate any new information into what is already known within the organisation (*the integration of new information into the organisational context*). The next task for the organisation is to ascribe meaning to the new learning, that is, organisational members have to share and explore their perceptions in order to arrive at a shared interpretation (*the collective interpretation of information*). The final task for the organisation is to empower organisational members to experiment with the new learning and this kick-starts a new learning cycle (*empower staff to take responsible action based on the interpreted meaning*).

It is obvious from the list of tasks above that implementing organisational learning strategies is not an easy task and that both time and effort would have to be invested in order to have systems that are robust enough to bring about some real organisational benefits. Having said that, there is no reason why organisations that do not currently have much in the way of formal organisational learning mechanisms could not start in a small way by implementing organisational learning mechanisms for their project management activities. This would increase the chances of the projects being successful and would save money overall, given the relatively high cost of failed projects.

How Can Organisations Learn From Projects?

There are many ways in which organisations could learn from projects; however, we will stay with the framework provided by Dixon (1994) and look at what could be done to enable greater and systematic learning from projects.

THE WIDESPREAD GENERATION OF INFORMATION

By using the word 'information' in this context, Dixon (1994) is referring not only to external information ('explicit' information) but also the thoughts and ideas that are generated internally within each individual ('tacit' information). One of the building blocks for learning from projects is finding out a wide range of information about the subject of the project, the project itself and the impact on stakeholders and the organisation. In most projects, this will already happen to some degree so it may just be that the existing process needs to cast its nets a little wider or a little deeper in order to generate a sufficient depth and breadth of information.

There are also several new considerations in this 'gathering of information' process that probably do not exist in current projects. Firstly, there is the need for each person within the project (including stakeholders) to take responsibility for generating information from their areas that they come into contact with or are aware of. This responsibility will need to be communicated, clarified and well understood amongst project team members/stakeholders. Secondly, the generation of information, as mentioned in the previous point, needs to cross established organisational barriers, that is, it should not be restricted to any organisational boundaries. Friedlander (1984) comments that:

Organisational learning occurs at the interfaces between persons, between organisational units and between the organisation and its external environment.

This gathering of information from a wide range of sources by a range of people provides a rich source of information and perspectives which can be harnessed to inform existing and future projects. A final point is that the collection of information needs to be continuous to reflect ongoing changes in various processes and environments.

INTEGRATING NEW INFORMATION INTO THE ORGANISATIONAL CONTEXT

It is all well and good having a system for the ongoing collection of information but this is not going to have any impact on the quality of projects unless there are processes in place to utilise that information on a continuous basis. The information collected by each project member/stakeholder will need to be shared with all parties and reviewed to see what implications there are for the project. Some of the information will also need to be documented for future reference. There are many possible ways in which this could be achieved. One relatively easy way to store and share this emerging information would be to have a shared website where people input information relevant to the project. All project members and stakeholders could than have access to this site. Even better, the site could be accessible to all organisational members so that they can add any information or insights that they are able to offer. In conjunction with this, you could add a 'learning log' to your range of project documents and this could be used to record any new learning that you think would be useful for the future or to keep an audit trail of events that have influenced decision/direction changes.

PREVENT DEFENSIVE ROUTINES

There are some pitfalls to be aware of with this process of collating information into the organisational context. Defensive routines can come into play. Daft and Huber (1987) suggest that the distribution of information can be obstructed in four ways: message routing, message summarising, message delay and message modification.

Message routing – is the selective routing of information. This can occur for any number of reasons; for example, the sender is not sure who the information is useful for or the sender may be deliberately avoiding sending the information to certain people. Having a central storage point for this information that is visible to everyone will help avoid this potential defensive routine.

Message summarising – as the name suggests, this is where a message is reduced in size which can have an impact on the quality of the information distributed. Information that would be significant to a third party may be unintentionally or intentionally omitted, for example by reducing a large set of numbers to averages. This can be avoided to some extent by adding a line to your guidelines which says that people should add raw information along with a summary so that others can investigate in further detail if they so wish.

Message delay – this can have a detrimental impact on the whole information generation/integrating process because important information could be sitting on someone's desk until it is too late to act. Project members and stakeholders will need to be advised to submit information as soon as is feasibly possible as it is important that information shared is timely.

Message modification – this is where the information is misreported or is given a particular slant which is misleading to others. This can occur for a number of reasons, for example, to avoid revealing negatives or failures. It is difficult to avoid downright deceit but ensuring that everyone is clear about the purpose of the information and that learning can best take place when the information is presented without bias will help avoid such practices. It will also be necessary to have some ground rules about how people respond to information that they see on your shared site, for example not criticising but being respectful of others, and so on. In other words, as we have discussed in previous chapters, it is necessary to create a culture and environment of trust and collaboration, otherwise learning will not take place and the established learning mechanisms will become pointless routine processes.

COLLECTIVELY INTERPRETING THE INFORMATION

It is important to remember that this is a stage in the organisational learning cycle and needs to have the same attention dedicated to it as the other stages, if not more. Within organisations, people often assume that if information is available on an intranet or in a missive that has been sent round, then people will have read it and remembered it. This is a nice idea but it does not tend to work in practice. We have all been guilty of ignoring various organisational missives either because we did not have the time to look at them or because they did not generate any interest for us. In other words, it is dangerous to assume.

In order for organisational learning to occur, organisational members must not only read and remember the information, they must also discuss it with others. It is only by sharing different perspectives and exploring the implications that we reach any sort of shared understanding and learning takes place. This may sound a little odd, however, when we examine human behaviour in its everyday context; for example, when looking at 'real-life problem-solving situations we see a certain set of cognitive processes. People within organisations tend to 'think in conjunction or partnership with others and with the help of culturally provided tools and implements' (Salomon 1993: xiii). That is to say that the way in which people think about things in organisations is influenced by the people around them and the culture and climate of the organisation.

Agreement and understanding about information emerge in situations where teams of people work together to solve organisational problems.

Once again for this to happen it is necessary to ensure that people are reminded to review information on the shared site at frequent intervals. In addition, it may be worth encouraging discussion threads on the site so that people will seek shared meaning from the new information. It is even better if face-to-face discussions can be arranged as this allows for a more natural discussion and exchange of ideas in which emotions can be more accurately interpreted. If information emerges that is of particular relevance to the project then a meeting could be arranged to discuss it and a number of project team members and stakeholders could be invited to attend. When important meetings are held or important decisions made, time should be specifically included to critique and learn from these events.

Dixon (1994) suggests that there are three core values that enhance collective collaboration:

- *Freedom* – being able to speak openly without worrying that you will be criticised or punished in some way.

- *Equality* – being able to speak your mind regardless of rank. This is a prerequisite for freedom.

- *Respect* – mutual respect is very important as a basis for freedom.

Dixon's view is very much in keeping with what we have discussed so far about the importance of creating the right atmosphere for trust and sharing. Interestingly, Dixon (1994) suggests that the reason that organisations do not learn is because they are unable/unwilling to create environments where freedom, equality and respect coexist. I doubt that the explanation of why organisations don't learn is that simplistic but there is no question that the culture and environment of the organisation play a crucial part in determining how and if an organisation learns. The same is true of project teams.

AUTHORITY TO TAKE RESPONSIBLE ACTION BASED ON THE INTERPRETED MEANING

The final stage (within this organisational learning cycle bearing in mind that the end of one cycle kick-starts another) is to empower project team members and stakeholders to act on their learning. This is probably best achieved through not being too prescriptive on how actions are completed or how decisions are made. If actions are too prescriptive then there is no room for flexibility or change based on the organisational learning that has been achieved.

A word of caution

If you are a project manager delivering a project in an organisation that does not have any learning processes in place, be aware that the success of any learning processes that you put into place for your project may be impacted by the organisational environment. Although projects can sometimes look and feel like totally separate entities, in reality, they are not. They are simply sub-systems of a bigger entity and although different processes and procedures can operate within a project, there may be difficulties at the boundaries with the wider organisation. This should not deter you from implementing organisational learning processes but you may have to be slightly less ambitious about what you can achieve.

Don't despair; even if you are delivering a project in an organisation that is not interested in organisational learning, there is still learning to be had. Most organisations will keep some records of previous projects and you should be able to learn something from the records about where these projects were successful and where less so. In addition, you can still encourage your project team to implement some basic organisational learning processes.

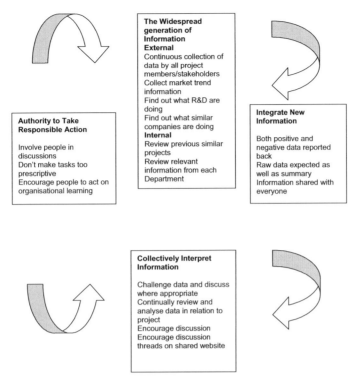

Figure 11.2   A brief example of an organisational learning cycle for a project

Attitudes of Leaders Towards Both Failure and Learning

We have already looked at the contribution that organisational culture and climate make towards organisational learning and given that leaders shape the culture of the organisation, it is worth just saying a few words about them.

In Chapter 2, we looked at the different types of leadership models and it is clear that certain types of leader are more likely to successfully facilitate organisational learning than others. We have discussed the fact that some of the prerequisites for organisational learning to happen are around creating trusting atmospheres where organisational members feel equal, respected and comfortable in expressing their views without fear of being castigated in any way. We have also talked about the fact that in order to achieve organisational learning it is necessary to have a good degree of challenge, which means that it is necessary for any leader to be able to build a shared vision that involves constantly challenging and questioning the status quo.

Based on our discussion in Chapter 2, the types of leadership that would perhaps best facilitate organisational learning are 'transformational' leadership with its emphasis on creating vision and trust along with empowering organisational members to act. In addition, 'transformational' leaders accept and are comfortable with taking risks. This element of risk is something that we have not yet discussed within the concept of organisational learning; however, it is a significant topic that is worthy of some discussion. Just refer back to our discussion earlier in this chapter around empowering staff to take responsible action with their new organisational learning. When staff are empowered to take individual responsibility in organisations, this can increase the risk or can be perceived as increasing the risk. Some types of leadership prefer order and specified control mechanisms. In addition, these types of leaders are probably quite risk-averse. They would probably be very uncomfortable and possible even stressed at the thought of staff members/project members making their own decision based on organisational learning.

In addition, both 'emotionally intelligent' leadership and 'authentic' leadership also emphasise an atmosphere of trust and staff empowerment. The earlier forms of leadership such as 'situational' leadership are less likely to be successful in facilitating sustained organisational learning. This is because their focus is very much on task and process which is helpful in terms of designing and implementing processes to facilitate learning. At the same time, however, they are less likely to focus on interrelationships and boundaries, which is where most organisational learning takes place.

An additional point of interest is that Kolb (1984) carried out some research with a range of leaders and found that most of them had a personal learning style which was action-oriented. Kagan (1996) found that very active orientations towards learning situations inhibit reflection and therefore preclude the development of analytic concepts. Consequently, as well as a focus on their leadership style, it is necessary for leaders to be aware of their own personal learning style and how that impacts on the type of leadership style that they utilise.

QUESTIONS FOR REFLECTION

1.   How will you ensure that you collect an appropriately wide and comprehensive body of knowledge about your project on an ongoing basis?

2.   How will you evaluate and record this knowledge/experience including any perceived failures?

3.   How will you ensure that this knowledge/experience is available to those in the organisation who may need it, at the point which they need it?

4.   How will you maintain and sustain these processes?

12

Project Wind-Down

Often as a project starts to wind down, the project manager's only concern appears to be the 'end of project' report and the 'signing off' by the project board. These are important considerations but they are not the ones that a good project manager should have. The end of a project can be a triumph and a release because once again you have delivered the impossible; however, there will be other emotions at play.

The project team are likely to be disbanding and returning to their day jobs or they may be moving to a new job or even leaving the organisation to take up a new role. This is particularly true of the longer-term projects where people are seconded to the project for so long that returning to their original job ceases to be an option, for a variety of reasons. The dissolution of the project team is likely to result in a range of emotions amongst project team members and these emotions need to be managed effectively.

Emotions tend to be more prominent when the project has not been a success and it is perhaps these situations that should merit the most attention. The failure of a project within an organisation, particularly a large or longer-term one, is rarely private and it is probable that most people in the organisation will have heard of its failure. This situation can lead to team members feeling demoralised and demotivated. They may even have concerns about their wider careers within the organisation and their chances of obtaining future promotion. This is true even when the project failure cannot be attributed to any particular individual. No one likes to be associated with failure and people can get 'tarred with the same brush'. It is important that the project team is supported through this time, and there are steps that a project manager can take to ease the situation for the project team.

Managing the Emotions of Team Members

In Chapter 9 we talked about the types of reactions that people can have to change, and the end of a project can be perceived as a fairly significant change by people, particularly where people may have worked on a project for many months or even years. In some cases team members are about to lose their 'job', their 'manager' and their 'team' so it is not surprising there is often a sense of loss. Team members are likely to experience some of the emotions and feelings that we discussed in Chapter 9 and their emotions may go through the various phases we discussed: denial, bargaining, depression and acceptance. These emotions will vary in intensity from one individual to another and it is important to remember that, for some team members, these emotions could start to have a detrimental effect on their well-being and therefore must be addressed.

It is important that the project manager is mindful of team member's emotions and identifies any team members who appear to be experiencing higher levels of emotion as these individuals may require more one-to-one support than others. Overall, though, there will be a need to acknowledge these emotions and take action to manage them. Possible actions include interventions at the team level and interventions at an individual level and there may be a need to take action at both levels, depending on the strength of emotions that the team is displaying and the extent to which any individual team members appear to be experiencing particular difficulties.

INDIVIDUAL INTERVENTIONS

One action that the project manager can instigate at an individual level is to have a one-to-one discussion with each team member (which may need to take place by telephone if there are remote team members or if the project team is global). The focus of the discussion should be to explore how the team member is feeling and to ascertain what support they feel that they need to make their next transition, which may be returning to their job or may be starting a new role. This is very much an element of 'good practice' and should always form part of the project wind-down for longer-term projects as it helps people to accept the loss of the project and move on positively. Often there is practical support that people need in order to move on, for example a reference or even assistance in finding a new role. Consequently, it is worth having conversations with team members at the start of the wind-down process as opposed to waiting until the end, so that there is time to instigate any practical support that may be required. If there are team members who are concerned about their next role, it would be worth involving your HR department and asking them to assist your team members in finding their next move.

TEAM-LEVEL INTERVENTIONS

It is important from both a practical and a psychological perspective that the project is reviewed by the team to explore which actions and behaviours were successful, which were less so and which were unsuccessful. The practical benefit of this type of in-depth review is that it contributes to the individual learning of the project team and helps them to understand their own development needs with regard to future projects or roles. These development needs could be about knowledge gaps, working on projects or even be about how best to work in a team environment or with stakeholders. In addition, the information that emerges from this project review will contribute to organisational learning and will add additional depth to any organisational learning processes that you have already put in place to capture information and learning from the project. It is important that the emerging information is documented and shared with any relevant parties in order to facilitate maximum organisational learning.

The psychological benefit of reviewing the project is that it helps team members understand the reasons for any failure and attribute them correctly to the actual causes of failure so that they do not feel that they have failed personally. In addition, from an individual perspective, there needs to be a second dimension to this process around boosting or maintaining team morale. In Chapter 3, we talked about using positive psychology with teams to manage negative events and if your project has been less than successful, this may be a good time to utilise some of the techniques that we discussed. We discussed the fact that it was detrimental to team morale to keep referring back to earlier failures. Consequently, the project manager will need to manage the discussion so that it remains upbeat and motivating. This is not always easy when reviewing projects as there will inevitably always be something that did not work as well as you hoped or expected. This means that the project manager will need to plan in advance how he is going to manage the low points of the discussion. There are ways of doing this. After discussing an action or aspect of the project that did not work too well, in order to avoid the team feeling low, the project manager can shift the focus to exploring what they learned from it and how they would use that learning in the future. This gets people into planning mode and helps avoid the low mood associated with aspects of the project that were less successful or unsuccessful. It is important also (as we said in Chapter 3) not to dwell for long on the failures but to acknowledge the learning from them and move on. It is important also that the discussion should end with the positives so that everyone leaves feeling that they have achieved something. Remember the concept of 'Gratitude' that we discussed in Chapter 3, whereby you ask team members to identify five things that they are grateful for. This also provides an opportunity to identify the successes that you achieved, that is, the things that did go well in the project.

Communication

It is important that information about the project is shared so that everyone is clear about what was successful and what was not. This is part of any organisational learning process and is good practice. The purpose of the communication is twofold: firstly it shares the learning from the project, and secondly, where the project has not been successful, it should be used to explain the reasons for the failure so that no blame is attached to individuals within the project team. When communicating to the organisation en masse, it is important to draft your message carefully and preferably have a colleague read it before you publish it. This is important, particularly where a project has not been successful, because you need to ensure that the tone of the message as open, honest and upbeat as it can be. You will also need to ensure that there is no hint of blame attached to any particular individual or group within the organisation as this can lead to ill feeling and conflict.

It is likely that you will need to communicate information about the project at different levels and possibly in different ways. Obviously, you will have carried out a review with your team. It is helpful, however, to have meetings with primary stakeholders to discuss the overall progression of the project and learn from the stakeholders what they think worked well and what didn't. You can also share your observations of their contribution and whether or not there were times in the project where you would have benefited from something additional (or different) from them. This also helps build up an organisational picture of what worked and what did not and is essential information for planning future projects. It is also useful information to share with your project team to aid their understanding of why some things were not as successful as they might have been or indeed why something was as successful as it was. This will also be useful information to include in your final project report to the project board.

Sustaining Changes Made by the Project

This phase in the project is a good time to review the support mechanisms that you have put in place to sustain the change that you have completed throughout the phases of the project. In Chapter 9 we talked about Field of Forces and how it was important to identify and work with the drivers for and against change. It would be worth reviewing your scoping phase at this point to ensure that you have sufficient drivers in place to sustain the changes that your project has brought about and that there are mechanisms in place to manage and minimise any forces against the change.

There will be a need to communicate with all parties who have a role to play in sustaining the changes, for example the senior team, to ensure that everyone is clear about the actions that they will need to take on an ongoing basis in order to maintain the change and prevent people slipping back into old ways of doing things. It is worth meeting key people on a one-to-one basis in order to find out about any concerns that they may have and to ensure that everyone is feeling supported in going forward. This provides a good opportunity for you to ensure that they have a plan in place to make sure everything happens in support of the change and that they have actions with milestones and review points.

A bigger challenge in maintaining the change process is ensuring that managers and staff continue to work in the new ways that you have implemented. Communication and training are vital tools in this process and it would be worth ensuring that there are clear instructions for any new ways of working and that any older instructions or manuals are destroyed to eliminate any chances of confusion. It would also be helpful as part of your end of project communication to remind people of the changes and what you need them to continue doing in order to support the project.

Training

It is important to remember that even if you have provided training in the new ways of working throughout the project, there may be a need for further training if staff are still not totally clear about what they should be doing. You will also need to have a plan in place for how new people should be trained and inducted. This is important because you need to ensure that newcomers learn only the new ways of working and are not taught any bad habits. This will help reinforce the changes that you have brought about because, over time, the changes that you have implemented will become the norm.

QUESTIONS FOR REFLECTION

1.   Do you have a plan to manage team emotions during the project wind-down?

2.   Have you allocated time to reflect on and explore how the project went and any implications for the future?

3.   Have you allocated time to communicate project successes and learning points to the wider organisation?

4.   Have you identified whether team members will need support in returning to their jobs or in finding a new post within (or outside) the organisation?

5.   Is everyone clear about their role once the project ends in order to sustain any changes that have been brought about?

Summary

For human beings organisational change is a psychological journey with many twists and turns, as opposed to a direct route to a different way of working.

We have covered a range of project-related topics in this book and we have looked at aspects of psychology that could help make these processes more successful. We have looked at the skills needed for project management and the types of skills that you might need from your project team. We have also looked at ways of building a successful culture within your project team and how best to lead that team. We looked at the role that coaching can play both for project teams and for stakeholders and we have also looked at ways of engaging project team members and the wider stakeholder group.

We have examined the human elements to consider when producing and delivering your project communication plan and we have explored the contribution that individual personality makes to an individual's willingness to take appropriate risks. We have also explored the issue of conflict and how it can be used positively to facilitate project learning.

In Chapter 9, we looked at change management and the fact that most modern-day projects result in organisational change for some (if not all) groups within organisations, which means that project managers are essentially change managers. We have also looked at some practical tips on how best to manage the project board and use it as a resource. The final stage of the book looked at the latter phases of a project, that is, what has been learned from it and how best to manage the wind-down of the project.

Underlying Themes

Throughout this book, there has been common themes around many of the processes that we have discussed, for example building a team, engaging stakeholders, communicating, and so on and those themes have been around:

1. *Relationship-building* – building strong relationships that promote effective interpersonal relationships.

2. *Building shared ownership* – being democratic and open to suggestions. Seeking the views of others and valuing their opinions regardless of whether you agree with them.

3. *Building understanding* – reaching a shared understanding of what is important and how to achieve it.

4. *Creating a mutual vision* – engaging and motivating people by sharing your vision and enthusiasm.

5. *Creating harmonious relationships* – looking to build peace and harmony in order to facilitate good working relationships. This does not mean avoiding conflict but using it productively (where it occurs) in order to achieve harmony.

Underlying Psychological Skills and Approaches

Despite the fact that the topics covered so far have been quite different, there appears to be a set of underlying psychological skills and approaches which, when utilised effectively, are more likely to be significant in facilitating project success than some of the more traditional skills and approaches required of a project manager; most project managers, for example, are good at organising, planning and delivering objectives to agreed timescales. These skills are very important to project management; however, they are not enough on their own to facilitate project success and it is necessary for project managers to also have a range of psychological skills and approaches in their toolkit.

There is a psychological basis to the 'underlying themes' mentioned above and there are certain underlying skills that provide a good foundation to assist project managers in being able to deliver the activities referred to in the previous paragraph on 'underlying themes'.

Underlying Psychological Skills and Approaches

HONESTY AND OPENNESS

Honesty and openness are about being comfortable in sharing information and feelings with others and making a conscious effort to do so (appropriately). They also involve trusting others, for example trusting that people have the ability to deliver a task or trusting that what they say is true. I am not advocating that we all trust each other blindly – a certain degree of scepticism is usually quite healthy; however, it is important to try to foster environments where people feel trusted and safe and where they feel that they can trust you. Project managers, like other managers, sometimes refrain from sharing information, particularly bad news, in case it harms team morale. Unfortunately for managers, team members are usually fairly intelligent and are usually aware when all is not going well. Consequently, when information is withheld, however well-intentioned, it can create feelings of mistrust.

ACTIVE LISTENING

In Chapter 4 we talked about the different types of listening that we all routinely engage in and unfortunately most of it is not of the 'active listening' variety. This is a great shame because real listening (that is, paying a higher degree of attention not only to what someone is saying but how they are saying it) is potentially a very powerful tool. Active listening enables us to have a deeper understanding of someone else and what their concerns are. This enables us to gain a better understanding with regard to someone's strengths and abilities and how best to relate to them and interact with them. It also enables the other party in the conversation to feel that they are 'listened to' and understood. They feel that someone is paying them attention and consequently feel valued, which helps increase morale.

EMPATHY

Empathy is about being able to step out of your own framework of opinions and being able to appreciate things from someone else's point of view. It is about not being judgemental. It is also about being able to share someone else's emotional experience.

AN UNDERSTANDING OF THE ROLE THAT PERSONALITY FACTORS PLAY

There are a number of chapters in this book where we have looked at the value that understanding something about the personalities of the team can add to managing a project. I think that there is a need for project managers to take time to gain as much of an understanding as possible of the project team's personality predispositions and to then utilise this information (along with information around individual competencies and confidence) to allocate tasks and decision-making responsibility. Project managers will not often be in a position where psychometric personality profiles are available for their team members. Consequently, it is important that project managers take the time to get to know their team members at a deeper level as opposed to the superficial level that managers are often satisfied with.

USING EMOTIONAL INTELLIGENCE

In Chapter 2, we talked about 'emotionally intelligent leadership' and it would be useful at this stage to look at some of the underlying skills associated with this and why they could be of value to a project manager. 'Emotional intelligence' is about recognising emotions and knowing when and how to express emotion and being able to manage it. This is a really useful skill to have when interacting with people because if you are aware that you are experiencing anger or frustration, you can start to examine why you feel that way instead of letting your emotions run away with you. This avoids behaving in a way that could potentially impact on the harmony of the relationship or the trust that you have worked to establish. The other part of 'emotional intelligence' is about 'social competence' and this is the ability to tune into the emotions of others and use this information to facilitate good relationships and effective communication. It is easy to see how having a higher level of 'emotional intelligence' would help with the underlying themes that we referred to earlier in this chapter.

BEING MINDFUL

Be aware and mindful of team processes/team interactions. When you are interacting with your project team members/stakeholders either in a one-to-one capacity or in a meeting, do not just pay attention to the content of the conversation. In Chapter 6, we talked about the non-verbal aspects of communication and the fact that it provides us with a great deal of additional information about the speaker(s) and how they really feel and think about things. Being mindful of processes/interactions can be really valuable for a project manager and help him gain a deeper understanding of what is really going on for project team members and stakeholders.

It is also important for project managers to be mindful of their own prejudices and stereotypes so that they can be aware of when they are coming into play and ensure that they are not unduly influenced by them.

BEING RESPECTFUL

Being respectful is not about the general courtesies of interaction such as saying 'Please' and 'Thank you', nor is it about being deferential to people more senior than you. Being respectful is about having positive regard for other people and being prepared to listen to them (active listening) and understand their viewpoint (empathy). Being respectful in all dealings with the project team and stakeholders will help engender an environment of trust and support.

Psychological Tools

Throughout the book there has been some reference to various psychological tools:

- The Belbin questionnaire

- Psychometric personality questionnaires (for example, Wave, OPQ, 16PF)

- The MBTI

- The 'signature strengths indicator'

- The managerial grid

- The OK corral

- The 'Grow' model

- The 'Firo B' model of inter-relationships

- 'Emotional intelligence' questionnaires, for example Baron EQI

These are just examples of the many psychologically based tools available that could help project managers create strong relationships in their projects. The majority of the tools mentioned are freely available whilst others such as the 'personality questionnaires' require a trained and qualified practitioner to deliver and interpret them. Many HR departments have staff who are trained to use these tools and it would be helpful for project managers to build good relationships with the HR department.

Further Developing Your Psychological Approach?

The secret to development is self-awareness in that, if you are aware of your current level of functioning with regard to the underlying psychological skills and approaches mentioned overleaf, you will be able to identify your personal skill/knowledge gaps. Once you have achieved this, you will be able to look at ways of further developing your ability to utilise psychological skills and approaches.

There are many different ways in which you could further hone your skills, and the best methods will be the ones that are compatible with your particular learning style and your training budget. There are a few suggestions listed below, some of which incur little or no cost and some of which would require a more significant financial investment. It is generally more effective to use a selection of methods in order to develop both skills and knowledge.

A FEW SUGGESTIONS

- Read more and do not be afraid to experiment with new techniques.

- Find a coach who can help you identify your comfort zones and support you in challenging them as you extend your repertoire of interaction styles.

- Find a mentor with experience of delivering successful projects and utilise their experience of managing the 'softer' side of projects to guide you.

- Seek feedback from colleagues and team members with regard to your current styles of interaction/leadership.

- Find a good role model for the types of behaviours that you would like to emulate and observe how they do things.

Further Reading

Briggs Myers, I. (2000). *Introduction to Type*. 6th Edition. USA: CPP.

Caruso, D. (2004). *The Emotionally Intelligent Manager: How to Develop and use the Four Key Emotional Skills of Leadership*. San Francisco: Jossey-Bass.

Jongeward, D. (1976). *Everybody Wins: A Transactional Approach to Organisations*. New York: Addison-Wesley Publishing.

Lee, G. (2003). *Leadership Coaching*. London: CIPD.

Northouse, P.G. (2010). *Leadership Theory and Practice*. 5th Edition. London: Sage.

Toplis, J., Dulewicz, V. and Fletcher, C. (1997). *Psychological Testing: A Manager's Guide*. London: Institute of Personnel and Development.

References

Ackoff, R.L. (1994). *The Democratic Corporation: A Radical Prescription for Recreating Corporate America*. Oxford: Oxford University Press.

Anastasi, A. (1990). *Psychological Testing*. 6th Edition. New York: Macmillan Publishing Company.

Argrys, C. and Schon, D.A. (1996). *Organizational Learning 11*. Addison Wesley.

Bachman, W. (1988). Nice Guys Finish First: A SYMLOG Analysis of US Naval Commands. In Polleu, R.D. (ed.), *The SYMLPG Practitioner: Applications of Small Group Research*. New York: Praeger.

Barker, D. (1980). *TA and Training: The Theory and Use of Transactional Analysis in Organisations*. Farnham: Gower Publishing.

Barrezeele, K. (2000). Seventy Per Cent of Projects Fail to be Delivered Successfully. *De fiancieel-Economische Tijd*. Belgium. 31 March.

Barrick, M.R. and Mount, M.K. (1991). The Big Five Personality Dimensions and Job Performance: A Meta Analysis. *Personnel Psychology*. 44, 1–25.

Belbin, M. (1991). *Management Teams: Why They Succeed or Fail*. Oxford: Butterworth-Heinemann Ltd.

Blake and Moutons. (1966). In Luthans, F. (1989). *Organisational Behaviour*. 5th Edition. Singapore: McGraw Hill International Editions.

Breslin, J.W. and Rubin, J.Z. (1991). *Conflict Analysis and Resolution: Theory and Practice*. New York: Penguin Books.

Briggs Myers, I.B. (2000). *Introduction to Type*. Oxford: OPP.

Briner, W., Hastings, C. and Geddes, M. (1996). *Project Leadership*. 2nd Edition. Farnham: Gower Publishing.

Burnes, B, (1992). *Managing Change*. London: Pitman Publishing.

Burns, J. (1978). *Leadership*. New York: Harper and Row.

Cleland, D.L. and King, W.R. (1983). *Systems Analysis and Project Management*. 3rd Editition. New York: McGraw-Hill.

Csikszentmihalyi, M., Abuhamdeh, S. and Nakamura, J. (2005). Flow. In Elliot, A.J. and Dweck, C.S. (eds), *Handbook of Competence and Motivation*. New York: Guildford Press.

Daft, R.L. (1983). *Organisation Theory and Design*. West St Paul, Minnesota.

Daft, R.L. and Huber, G.P. (1987). How Organisations Learn: A Communication Framework. *Research in the Sociology of Organisations*. No 5, pp. 1–36.

Dixon, N. (1994). *The Organizational Learning Cycle: How We Can Learn Collectively*. London: McGraw-Hill.

Fisher, R. and Ury, W. (1999). *Getting to Yes: Negotiating an Agreement Without Conflict*. New York: Penguin Books.

Fisher, R., Ury, W. and Patton, B. (1991). *Getting to Yes: Negotiating an Agreement Without Giving in*. Random House. 2nd Edition. London: Business Books.

Friedlander, F. (1984). In Dixon, N. (1994), *The Organizational Learning Cycle: How We Can Learn Collectively*. London: McGraw-Hill.

Furnham, A. (2000). *Body Language at Work*. London: Chartered Institute of Personnel and Development.

Furnham, A. and Gunter, B. (1993). *Corporate Assessment: Auditing a Company's Personality*. London: Routledge.

Gable, S.L. and Haidt, J. (2005). What (and Why) Is Positive Psychology? *Review of General Psychology*. 9, 103–110.

Galway, T. (1974). *The Inner Game of Tennis*. New York: Random House.

Gibson, C.B. and Cohen, S.G. (2003). *Virtual Teams that Work: Creating Conditions for Virtual Team Effectiveness*. John Wiley & Sons.

Gok, W.Y. (1997). *Organisational Culture, Gender and Management of Project Teams*. Thesis. UMIST, Manchester.

Goleman, D., Boyatzis, R. and McKee, A. (2002). *The New Leaders*. London: Little, Brown.

Hay McBer. (1997). *Competency Study Database*. October. Boston. Reported in Goleman, D. and Cherniss, C. (2001). San Francisco: Jossey-Bass.

Hersey, P., Blanchard, K. and Johnson, D. (2009). *Management of Organisational Behaviour: Leading Human Resources*. UK: Prentice Hall.

Higgs, M. and Dulewicz, V. (1999). *Making Sense of Emotional Intelligence*. Berkshire: ASE.

Hofstede, G. (1980). *Culture's Consequences: International Differences in Work Related Values*. Newbury Park: Sage.

Huse, E.F. (1980). In Burnes, B., (1992). *Managing Change*. London: Pitman Publishing.

Hylväri, I. (2007). *Project Management Effectiveness in Different Organisational Conditions*. Helsinki School of Economics.

Institute for Employment Studies. (2004).

Janis, I.L. (1972). *Victims of Groupthink*. Boston: Houghton Mifflin.

Jose, H.D. and Crumly, J.A. (1993). In Weigel, R. (2000), *Risk and Resilience in Agriculture: The Influence of Personality on Risk Management Decisions.* University of Wyoming. Article 6.4.

Kagan, D. In Starkey, K. (ed.) (1996). *How Organisations Learn.* London: International Thomson Business Press.

Keil, M. (1999). In Glass, R.L. (1999). *Computing Calamities: Lessons Learned from Products, Projects and Companies that Failed.* New Jersey: Prentice Hall.

Kelly, G.A. (1963). *A Theory of Personality. The Psychology of Personal Constructs.* US: Norton and Co.

Kharbanda, O.P. and Stallworthy, E.A. (1983). *How to Learn From Project Disasters: True Life Stories With a Moral for Management.* England: Gower.

Kolb, D.A. (1984). In Dixon, N. (1994). *The Organizational Learning Cycle: How We Can Learn Collectively.* London: McGraw-Hill.

Kouzes, J.M. and Posner, B. (1995). *The Leadership Challenge: How to Keep Getting Extaordinary Things Done in Organisations.* Jossey-Bass.

Kubler-Ross, E. (2005). *On Grief and Grieving: Finding the Meaning of Grief Through the Five Stages of Loss.* London: Simon & Schuster Ltd.

Lewicki, R.J., Barry, B. and Saunders, D.M. (2007). *Essentials of Negotiation.* 4th Edition. New York: McGraw-Hill, International Edition.

Lewin, K. in Burnes, B. (1992). *Managing Change.* London: Pitman Publishing.

Lientz, B.P. and Rea, K.P. (2000). *Project Management for the 21st Century.* 2nd Edition. London: Academic Press.

Linley, P.A. and Harrington, S. (2006). Playing to Your Strengths. *The Psychologist.* 19, 86–89.

Locke, E.A. and Latham, G.P. (1990). *A Theory of Goal Setting and Task Performance.* Englewood Cliffs, NJ: Prentice Hall.

Luthans, F. (1989). *Organisational Behaviour.* 5th Edition. Singapore: McGraw-Hill International Editions.

Makin, P. Cooper, C. and Cox, C. (1989). *Managing People at Work.* London: British Psychological Society and Routledge.

Margerison, C. and McCann, D. (1990). *TMS: An Overview.* TMS UK Ltd.

Meredith, J.R. and Mantel, S. (2003). *Project Management: A Managerial Approach.* John Wiley & Sons.

Moràn, R.B., Arlas, R.M. and Salguero, R.T. (2003). Risk Takers: Do They Know How Much of a Risk They are Taking? *Psychology in Spain.* vol. 7, no 1, 3–9.

Moxon, P. (1993). *Building a Better Team: A Handbook of Managers and Facilitators.* Farnham: Gower Publishing.

Mullins. (1989). In Furnham, A. and Gunter, B. (1993). *Corporate Assessment: Auditing a Company's Personality.* London: Routledge.

Nicholson, N., Fenton, O., Creevey, M., Soane, E. and Willman, P. (2002). *Risk Propensity and Personality*. London: ESRC.

Organizational Conditions. Boston Spa.

Papastamatiou, M. (2005). *Learning from Information System Project Abandonment: A Case Study*. Thesis. Manchester Business School.

Parsloe, E. and Wray, M. (2003). *Coaching and Mentoring: Practical Methods to Improve Learning*. London: Kogan Page.

Pinto, J.K., Thoms, P., Trailer, J., Palmer, T. and Govekar, M. (1998). *Project Leadership: From Theory to Practice*. Pennsylvania: Project Management Institute.

Posner. (1987). In Merdith, J.R. and Mantel, S. (2003). *Project Management: A Managerial Approach*. John Wiley & Sons.

Prince2 Project Manual. Office of Government and Commerce, UK.

Prochaska, J.O. and DiClemente, C.C. (1986). Towards a Comprehensive Model of Change. In N. Heather (ed.), *Treating Addictive Behaviors: Processes of Change*. New York: Plenum Press.

Reiss, G. (1992). *Project Management Demystified: Today's Tools and Techniques*. London: E. and F.N. Spoon.

Robinson, D., Perryman, S. and Hayday, S. (2004). *The Drivers of Employee Engagement*. Brighton, UK: IES.

Salomon, G. (1993). No Distribution Without Individual's Cognition: A Dynamic Interactional View. In G. Salomon (ed.), *Distributed Cognitions — Psychological and Educational Considerations*. Cambridge: Cambridge University Press, pp. 111–138.

Salovey, P. and Mayor, J.D. (1990). Emotional Intelligence, Imagination. *Cognition and Personality*. 9. 185–21.

Schein, E. (1993). Organizational Culture and Leadership. In Shafritz , J. and Ott, J.S. (eds) (2001). *Classics of Organization Theory*. Fort Worth: Harcourt College Publishers.

Schutz, W. (1994). *The Human Element. Productivity, Self-Esteem and the Bottom Line*. Jossey-Bass.

Seligman, M.E.P. (2004). *Authentic Happiness: Using the New Positive Psychology to Realize Your Potential for Lasting Fulfilment*. London: Nicholas Brealey Publishing.

Smith, M., Gregg, M. and Andrews, D. (1989). *Selection and Assessment: A New Appraisal*. UK: Pitman.

Starkey, K. (ed.) (1996). *How Organisations Learn*. London: International Thomson Business Press.

Stoner, J.A.F. (1968). Risky and Cautious Shifts in Group Decisions: The Influence of Widely Held Values. *Journal of Experimental Social Psychology*, 442–459.

Tanaka. (1996). In Starkey, K. (ed.) (1996). *How Organisations Learn*. International Thomson Business Press. London.

The Independent. (2009). Bad Planning to Blame for MoD Computer Delay. 15 January, p. 6.

The Standish Group Report: Chaos. (1995). The Standish Group.

Verma, V.K. (1995). *Managing the Project Team. The Human Aspects of Project Management*. vol. 3. USA: Project Management Institute.

Weigel, R. (2000). Risk and Resilience in Agriculture: The Influence of Personality on Risk Management Decisions. University of Wyoming. Article 6.4.

West, M. (1994). Effective Teamwork: Personal and Professional Development. London: British Psychological Society.

Whitmore, J. (2004). *Coaching for Performance*. London: Nicholas Brealey Publishing.

Woollams, S. and Brown, M. (1979). *The Total Handbook of Transactional Analysis*. Englewood Cliffs: Prentice-Hall.

Yukl. (2002). In Hylväri, I. (2007). *Project Management Effectiveness in Different Organisational Conditions*. Helsinki School of Economics.

Zimmerer, T. and Yasin, M.M. (1998). A Leadership Profile of American Project Managers. *Project Management Journal*. 29, 31–38.

Index

If you have found this book useful you may be interested in other titles from Gower

Accelerating Business and IT Change: Transforming Project Delivery
Alan Fowler and Dennis Lock
Hardback: 978-0-566-08604-5
CD-ROM: 978-0-566-08742-4

Change Leadership:
Developing a Change-Adept Organization
Martin Orridge
Paperback: 978-0-566-08935-0
e-book: 978-0-566-09243-5

Images of Projects
Mark Winter and Tony Szczepanek
Hardback: 978-0-566-08716-5

Making the Business Case:
Proposals that Succeed for Projects that Work
Ian Gambles
Paperback: 978-0-566-08745-5
e-book: 978-0-7546-9427-4

GOWER

Managing Group Risk Attitude
Ruth Murray-Webster and David Hillson
Hardback: 978-0-566-08787-5
e-book: 978-0-7546-8135-9

Project Leadership
Wendy Briner, Colin Hastings and Michael Geddes
Paperback: 978-0-566-07785-2

Project Politics:
A Systematic Approach to Managing Complex Relationships
Nita A. Martin
Hardback: 978-0-566-08895-7
e-book: 978-1-4094-1261-8

Project Success:
Critical Factors and Behaviours
Emanuel Camilleri
Hardback: 978-0-566-09228-2
e-book: 978-0-566-09229-9

Visit **www.gowerpublishing.com** and

- search the entire catalogue of Gower books in print
- order titles online at 10% discount
- take advantage of special offers
- sign up for our monthly e-mail update service
- download free sample chapters from all recent titles
- download or order our catalogue

#0020 - 230914 - C0 - 244/170/14 [16] - CB